China Currents

2012 Special Edition

China Currents

2012 Special Edition

James R. Schiffman and Penelope B. Prime, Editors

China Research Center, Atlanta, Georgia
www.chinacenter.net

Cover design: Vanessa F. Garver

For electronic browsing and ordering of this, and other China Research Center titles, visit www.chinacenter.net

For more information, please contact:
China Research Center
Atlanta, Georgia
info@chinacenter.net

China Currents: 2012 Special Edition
James R. Schiffman and Penelope B. Prime, Editors

ISBN: 978-0-9826415-2-1

Published in the United States by China Research Center

Design and Production: Carbon Press LC
Manufactured in the United States of America

First Edition

Contents

Preface vii

Change in Chinese Society

China's 80's Generation: Working for the Future 1
  Rory Zimmerman

Visualizing China in Transformation: The Underground and
  Independent Films of Jia Zhangke 10
  Shu-chin Wu

China's Higher Education Reform 15
  Guo-hua Wang

Differences in Willingness to Express One's Opinion in US and
  Chinese Online Consumer Interactions 21
  Wei Cai and Leigh Anne Liu

Economic Transition

China 2030: An Analysis of the World Bank's
  Reform Strategy. 29
  Zhenhui Xu

China's Response to U.S. Pressure to Revalue the RMB 34
  Lee Taylor Buckley

Understanding China's Trade Surplus: Going Beyond
  Currency Manipulation 42
  Sam Trachtman

Developing Western China: Xi'an's Maturing Economy and
  the Role of Producer Services 51
  Susan M. Walcott and Chen Ying

The Neoliberal Sunshine in Northwestern China: A Case Study of
  Government Sponsored Job Training Programs, Migration, and
  Poverty Alleviation in Gansu and Ningxia Provinces 55
  KuoRay Mao, Kay Kei Ho Pih and Shuming Bao

Business Environment

City and Rural Commercial Banks in China: The New Battlefield in
  Chinese Banking? 65
  Vijaya Subrahmanyam

New Words and Novel Usages: An Analysis of Marketing Vocabulary
Used by Chinese Online Shopping Websites 74
Hong Li and Shanshan Wang

Hong Kong and Macau: Two Dynamos in China's Pearl River Delta 85
Clifton W. Pannell

Soft Landings Curriculum for U.S.-China Entrepreneurship 93
Ye-Sho Chen, Edward Watson, and Renato Ferreira Leitão Azevedo

Manufacturing in China: The Key Decisions 109
An Interview with Scott Ellyson, CEO of East West Manufacturing, Inc.

International Relations

Manned Space Program and Making of Chinese National Identity. 116
Liang Yao

China and a U.S.-Iran War. 125
John Garver

China's Growing Presence in Latin America: Implications for U.S. and
Chinese Presence in the Region 130
Michael Cerna

Lee Teng-hui and Cross-Strait Relations: 1995-1999 140
Daniel S. Mojahedi

Vietnam's Relations with China: A Delicate Balancing Act. 147
Dennis C. McCornac

China's Increasingly Assertive Navalism 155
John Garver

About the Editors. 159

Preface

Economic reform and development in China are reshaping the global system in the 21st century and fueling an unprecedented social transition within China itself. *China Currents* is a forum for thoughtful, concise articles analyzing society in contemporary China, published as an online journal by the China Research Center at ChinaCurrent.com. Periodic special issues include selections from past issues, organized by topic. The 2012 Special Issue includes articles covering social change, economic transition, the business environment and international relations.

The Center would like to gratefully acknowledge financial support from East West Manufacturing as a Gold sponsor, and Keylingo Translations and Alcan as Silver sponsors. We would also like to thank Lisa Guthrie for her editorial contribution. The views expressed in these articles are those of the authors.

Founded in 2001, the China Research Center's mission is to promote understanding of greater China based on research and experience, and to work collaboratively on events and projects with the public and private sectors. The Center draws much if its expertise from the universities and institutions around the U.S. southeast, including Agnes Scott, the Carter Center, Dalton State, Emory, Georgia College & State University, Georgia Institute of Technology, Georgia State, Kennesaw State, Mercer, Oglethorpe, the University of Georgia and University of North Carolina at Greensboro. The Center is currently based at Georgia State University.

The associates of the Center believe that favorable U.S.-China relations will be critical to supporting economic development in the U.S. and greater China, and to promoting peace in the region. One of the foundations of favorable relations is mutual understanding based on knowledge and open communication. The associates specialize in the study of a wide variety of aspects of Chinese society, including language, culture, history, politics, society, international relations, demographics, geography, the environment, the economic system and the business environment. The Center's goal is to make knowledge and expertise available to a wide variety of constituents within and beyond our academic communities, as well as to enhance our academic work via cross-disciplinary and cross-institutional collaboration.

James R. Schiffman, Ph.D.
Penelope B. Prime, Ph.D.
November 2012

China's 80's Generation: Working for the Future

Rory Zimmerman
Vol. 1, No. 1
Fall 2010

Chinese born in the 1980's, known as 80 hou (baling hou in putong hua), are famous to Westerners as the first generation born during the enforcement of China's one-child policy. The 80 hou is a generation of more than 200 million only children with common burdens and opportunities. Their thinking is formed by traditional Chinese culture and Confucian morals, but they are beginning their careers in a nearly full-blown market guided by rules of the WTO. Many of them are single-handedly responsible for providing financially for their parents' retirement. As the 80 hou fulfill their responsibilities and accomplish their social goals, their unique perspective is sure to influence trends in the global economy.

For the past decade it has been in fashion to refer to the 80's cohort as the "little emperors," implying a generation of self-important only children who have chipped away at traditional Chinese filial piety with excessive demands for material goods that doting parents and grandparents are only too happy to provide. Indeed, some 80 hou in Beijing have lived up to the "little emperor" stereotype. Many come from families that gained wealth and residential property portfolios after receiving government reimbursement for vacating hutongs demolished to pave the way for Beijing's rapid urbanization. These families gained financial security by investing the reimbursements into newly developed apartments in the late 1990s, in some cases purchasing multiple units. As prices of apartments in Beijing escalated over the past ten years, many became set for life by cashing in one property while living in another, and renting a third unit to produce a stable income. Beijingers with such luck have been known to allow their only children to lead a leisurely existence. They can choose to work if they want to have more spending money, but there is no need for them to provide financially for themselves or their parents. However, this leisure class of fortunate 80 hou, said to have never tasted bitterness, represents a tiny sliver of the 80 hou demographic. The vast majority of the 80 hou honor their traditional role and work to carry out their responsibility within the family unit. As such, the majority of this generation is under serious pressure to fulfill the role of breadwinner for their families while at the same time attempting to advance in their careers and achieve their social goals.

80 hou remember the rarity of consumer goods throughout their formative years. China's economic transition was just getting under way, and scarcities created by central planning still prevailed. As a result, they are in tune with the anxieties of their elders' generation, prone to working long hours, and attentive to saving more than half of their monthly income. They also are the first generation to grow up exposed to Korean and American pop culture, and many are die-hard fans of Michael Jackson, *NSYNC and Guns N' Roses. But while they admire the boldness and free-spirited attitude of Westerners, their identity is ingrained by Chinese tradition. Educated 80 hou are well read in the Chinese classics, and they express great pride in their country. The 80 hou were shocked and appalled when they were first exposed to Western criticism in 2008 when the media highlighted protesters who defiled the 2008 Olympic Torch relay to China. Chinese 80 hou viewed with disdain the cultural tendency of French and other Western peoples to protest. Protesting in France is a political and cultural norm for communication between the people and the government, but this Western style did not translate well. Many Chinese found the protests absurd and offensive. In response, the 80 hou rallied together in online communities to express their great love of country and the dignity inherent in traditional Chinese culture. 80 hou also enjoy the ability to indulge in online shopping and entertainment. Fashion has become a passion for this generation, and the Louis Vuitton logo has made great inroads into 80 hou as a status symbol, yet they still recognize fine Chinese cuisine as the greatest luxury in the world.

As the 80 hou grew up, their education was the center of attention for grandparents and parents within the home. Everyone's resources were put toward advancing the child's education and skill. As young adults they were able to enter the workforce throughout a period of openness, which included China's acceptance into the WTO. Their first steps in establishing careers were taken during a period of economic boom. They have experienced greater opportunity at the start of their careers than most of the 90s generation probably will enjoy. The 90 hou are entering the workforce at a time of global economic recession. They do not remember past scarcities because their experiences have been shaped by a period of prosperous economic development and urbanization. However, the 90 hou may face more scarcity as adults entering the job market than the 80 hou.

80 hou are an important generation for their experience of entering the work-force at the moment when the Chinese economy became widely acknowledged as a driving force of the world market. Furthermore, 80 hou have come of age in an era of freedom to move, study, work and earn. Career advancement is obtainable in the modern market, but the tendency of young professionals to expect consistent praise, higher salaries or managerial positions--often cited as characteristic of America's Gen Y-- is antithetical to mainstream Chinese culture. While 80 hou have big dreams and high hopes for themselves, they are not likely to directly ask their bosses for new opportunities. Instead they pursue practical ways of preparing themselves for career advancement, like studying new skills or learning new trades.

Since Beijing has developed into a modern metropolis, millions of the 80s generation have migrated to the capital seeking better paying jobs and more access to international culture. This generation shares a common dream of home ownership, but the price of buying an apartment home in Beijing or Shanghai is so exorbitant that few can manage such a feat without financial contributions from their families. Average gross salaries for successful white-collar workers can range from 1,000 RMB to 3,000 RMB a month (about \$140 - \$400)[1].The going rate for residential property in Beijing is at least 16,900 RMB (\$2,500) per square meter[2], and the price of a 90 square meter apartment can be higher than 1.9 million RMB (\$279,400)[3]. The mainstream mindset of the 80 hou is to qualify for a good paying white-collar job, work long hours, and save most of one's income so as to eventually buy an apartment. The large rent-to-price ratio (approximately 1:546) does not deter people from pursuing investment in the real estate market or viewing it as a sound investment. The rent-to-price ratio compares the cost of renting a home to the cost of purchasing one. Buying a home is paramount because it meets the financial and social needs of adult Chinese today. After they buy a home, they can provide a place for their retired parents, marry and have a baby. Afterwards, savings will be directed towards giving their only child the best chance possible to succeed in education and career.

Tens of millions of the 80 hou are not white-collar professionals. They are young men and women who migrated from the countryside into China's major cities to work as servers in restaurants (fu wu yuan in putong hua) or guards at apartment complexes (bao an). They came from subsistence farming societies and moved to the eastern cities to earn a near subsistence wage. The meager salaries are saved to provide their families with health care. Illness can devastate these farm-

---

1   *Interview with Beijing local, Emily Wang.*
2   *"Beijing's housing prices dropped 8000 yuan" China Daily, By Cai Muyuan (chinadaily.com. cn) http://www.chinadaily.com.cn/bizchina/2010-05/11/content_9836345.html.*
3   *"Homebuyers reeling from Beijing property measures", Mon, May 17, 2010, AFP, http://www. asiaone.com/Business/News/Story/A1Story20100517-216615.html*

ing families. Middle-aged parents and young adult children work far from home all year, saving their salaries and pooling their earnings at Spring Festival family reunions. These working poor do not have enough money for a college education and do not qualify for white-collar jobs. They carry on a long-standing tradition of living for the next generation, which is an all-too-common experience for the peoples of developing nations. Parents work throughout their lifetimes, saving for basic nourishment and the advancement of their children's education. They do not entertain the idea that they will climb the social ladder themselves, but save their money to provide for family health care and direct their hopes toward the future of their progeny. For the 80 hou working poor, the menial jobs available in the city provide important perks such as free room and board. As the famous Chinese idiom proclaims: "To the people food is heaven." The migrant working poor of Beijing may earn an average of only a few hundred RMB a month, but they are able to save the majority of their pay for their families because rent and food are provided by their employers.

Despite the pressure to provide for their families and a high-level of competition for jobs and educational advancement, many individuals of the 80 hou pursue their career ideals with gusto. Three such individuals are profiled here. They come from a variety of backgrounds including highly educated families, subsistence farmers, and well-connected families. Each of the three has experienced times of scarcity and has suffered anxiety over finances, some more than others. What these three 80 hou share is their extraordinary attitude toward life in their quest to provide for their families while achieving their own goals. Each has taken whatever life presented and pursued individual social advancement. Each depends upon him or herself to provide financial security, and considers marriage a future prospect and not something to depend upon for social success. These three are not overcome by the pressure to provide, and they are far from complacent about their careers. In fact, they are passionate about fulfilling their ambitious dreams. Their individual stories follow.

Helen Zou

Helen Zou was born in a town southwest of Chongqing municipality. Her father was a well-known local lawyer and her mother a homemaker. In her youth, Helen assisted her father as a scribe, using her good handwriting to copy legal documents for his practice. Copy machines were a rarity, and when available, far too expensive. Her father was most impressed by her talent and intelligence. He encouraged her to pursue law or medicine, saying that a career as a lawyer, teacher or doctor was most suitable for women. She was intent upon following in her father's footsteps and studying law, but later, as his health failed, she wanted to become a doctor, so she could cure him of his ailments. However, he died the year before she was to choose a college major. Since she could no longer cure her father, she no longer found it practical to study medicine, and as her understanding of the red tape complexities of China's legal system grew, she gradually lost interest in pursuing a law degree.

Helen often read English novels and watched American movies. She had a great desire to travel to foreign countries. She remained at the top of her class throughout middle school and high school. When the time came to choose a college major, Helen chose English language. She graduated from Chongqing Three Gorges University in 2004, and had a secure job offer teaching English at Dalian University. She declined the offer and went to Beijing in search of more exposure to international culture. She started her work experience in Beijing as an employee of a Chinese state-owned company. In 2006, Helen began working as the assistant to an entrepreneur of a high-tech Chinese company preparing to make its IPO on NASDAQ. In this growing company she had the chance to participate in the functioning of projects from IPO to HR restructuring. Currently, she works for this company as an investor relations specialist. Helen enjoys being close to information, constantly aware of company affairs and industry trends. She recognizes the importance of delivering the right messages to investors. Her goal is to complete an MBA degree abroad to increase her understanding of finance and business ethics. Her career goal is to be the investor relations executive preparing Chinese companies for their IPOs on Western stock exchanges by overhauling their financial systems management and advertising these opportunities to investors.

Despite her strong work ethic and obvious talent in disseminating bilingual financial communication, she does not receive sufficient training for advancement opportunities from her company. Most booming Chinese companies have not yet developed a framework for conducting career mobility or training incentives for employees. The majority of employees in successful Chinese companies are content to have a secure job with decent pay in the big city. They do not feel the need to push for more opportunity. Those who are anxious to elevate their positions must constantly face the disappointment that their long hours and good efforts will not afford them advanced progression into managerial or decision-making roles. Helen is currently preparing for the TOEFL and GMAT examinations, studying in the evenings after work and on weekends. She will use her savings, accumulated over the last six years, to support her dream of studying abroad and attending an American university to complete her MBA degree. She must excel in these exams, since being awarded a scholarship by a foreign university is a financial imperative for her to accomplish her dream. As a 28-year-old, single woman in China, her career ambitions are countered by her responsibility to provide for her widowed mother. Helen must be able to afford her educational goals while providing for herself and her mother. The portion of her income not directed toward necessities and savings is spent trying her hand at the Chinese stock market. She views such investment as a hobby and not as a resource for financial gain. Such play enriches her experience in calculating risk in the Chinese stock market.

Helen considers marriage a future concern. Although she enjoys dating in her free time, she views such interaction as no more than interesting and fun. Helen believes that as she achieves her career goals, she will come into contact with a most suitable mate. She is certain he will be a dynamic individual with lots of international perspective. She looks forward to the day she can settle down with financial security and provide a stimulating home environment for her future family to thrive.

Yongbin Fang

Yongbin Fang was born to subsistence farmers in Anhui Province. His parents were born in the 1950s and as adolescents in the 1960s survived periods of starvation by chewing on seeds that they randomly found while sifting through the dust of the barren earth. Their parents, Fang's grandparents, were tormented by purges and eventually defeated by starvation. In the fertile 1980s, Fang was born into a family with survivors' spirit. He grew up helping his family reap the corn during the harvest season and attending the local school in the off-season. It was there that he gained literacy and studied basic mathematics. As a kid in the 1990s, he gazed wistfully at the skyscrapers towering off in the distance. Often the men of his village went to the city to work as construction laborers. They always returned home with cash for their families.

Fang dreamed of becoming an architect. At the age of 17, he left school and went to Suzhou to be a carpenter's apprentice. He worked for the whole year, learning the trade and earning only room and board. During the Spring Festival family reunion at the end of that year, his parents told him it was time to earn an income, so he followed his uncle and father to work as a carpenter on construction sites in burgeoning Beijing. Since he was young and nourished by his dream of becoming an architect, he proved to be a fast learner. The boss took notice of this and sent him to work as a mechanic at the garage he owned. There Fang mastered new trades and decided to invest in getting his driver's license. This new skill enabled him to earn a higher income by working as a bus driver for private kindergartens in Beijing. The savings he accumulated by working a better paying job was immediately invested into his educational advancement. He put himself through university while working full-time, earning a degree in interior design. The foreign English teachers working at the Beijing kindergartens often sought Fang's help and friendship. He realized the next useful skill for him to master was English language. So again he used his income to support his educational advancement. He completed an independent study program at Beijing Foreign Studies University and successfully passed all the exams to earn a diploma in English language and literature. He used his new skills by working as a translator for Chinese public relations firms, and prior to the 2008 Beijing Olympic Games he landed a job as a translator for a German news corporation that conducts all their China reporting in English, as it is more commonly spoken in China than German. He continues to adapt his skills to creatively strategize his financial security. Currently, he takes every opportunity to learn about professional photography so that he can advance his career into higher realms of the media industry.

In 2007, his parents and uncle combined their savings to help Fang purchase a small apartment in east Beijing. This investment provided Fang a secure living situation to support his career in Beijing. They hope that the money invested in the home purchase will prove to be an asset to them all in the future. Fang saves 80 percent of his monthly income to put toward basic necessities for his parents and himself in the future. His mother is still a housewife and subsistence farmer in the countryside. His father and uncle are migrant laborers who earn petty cash on construction sites. They are reaching the age of retirement, which to Fang means "forcibly jobless" because no one wants to hire elderly construction workers. He is not convinced the social insurance system will guarantee security for him and his family throughout their elderly years. The pension and subsidies directly accessible to his family are too low to rely upon in times of illness. Fang is responsible for providing for himself, his parents and his uncle over the next decades. Such responsibility leads to his high propensity to save, as well as hard work, will power and self-sacrifice. As his family has supported him, he will support them.

There is little time and few resources left for Fang to start a family of his own. Fang's peers in the hometown married in their early 20s and have raised large families. Fang has consistently resisted social pressures to fit in with his hometown peers and return there to marry a local girl. He centers his life on providing for his family and pursuing a professional career. He finds the girlfriends of his generation to be overly demanding. They require the suitor to own an apartment, and if that is achieved, then they chirp on about the location and quality of apartment necessary for them to agree to marriage. Men of the 80s generation must achieve a high level of material success to please the modern Chinese woman. Fang hopes to marry a woman with perspective and goals similar to his own. To afford such a wife and then have a child would be a privilege, but for now such a lifestyle is a luxury just out of his reach. At the age of 30, he still has plenty of time. Fang will continue to pursue his career ambitions and uphold his ideals for family life, making progress step-by-step. As the famous saying goes, a journey of a thousand "li" starts with a single step.

Candace Sun

Candace Sun was born in Anshan City, Liaoning Province. Her maternal grandfather was an engineer and her paternal grandfather a battalion commander in the Chinese Army. Her parents did well working in factories, and in the 1990s found success as small business owners. Candace's parents encouraged her to learn traditional Chinese arts and she excels at painting and calligraphy. Ever at the top of her class, she often won school competitions. In elementary school, she was the champion of an academic competition and was awarded a set of the four Chinese classics of literature. She cherished these great works and spent her free time reading the classics and learning other tales of Chinese philosophy.

In 2000, Candace was accepted into Beijing Wuzi University. There she earned a degree in economics. After graduating at the top of her class, she went to work full time at the company that had provided her college internship. She began working in the art department of a Chinese online gaming company as a professional 3D artist. Her skills in calligraphy and her knowledge of the classics and Chinese mythology were greatly appreciated by her employers. She provided real value to the company's product line, so once the company launched their IPO on NASDAQ, she was one of the original team members to be handsomely rewarded in stock options. Candace advanced to middle management leadership positions and received English language training from her company. Her ability to clearly express herself in English, and the value she contributes to the development of company product lines provides her more certain opportunity for career advancement.

In 2009, she put her assets into purchasing a fine apartment in one of Beijing's up-and-coming residential neighborhoods. She views home ownership as a long-term investment and as a way to provide for her parents' retirement. They live together in her apartment home, carrying for her nourishment as she fulfills the role of breadwinner. Candace's career goal is to become a senior professional manager for the company. She has successfully passed all graduate admissions examinations to enroll in the MBA program at the University of International Business & Economics in Beijing. She will attend graduate school part-time, while she continues to work full-time in the field of 3D design. She intends develop her skills to add value to her company's product line and is enthusiastic about contributing to making her company become one of the leading online game companies in the world. She enjoys her work and joyfully pursues her career. At 28 years old, she feels no pressure to marry anytime soon. She has a laissez-faire, or traditional Chinese Taoist wu-wei, go-with-the-flow attitude towards marriage. She has faith that a suitable partner will come into her life as she authentically pursues her dreams.

Conclusion

China's 80s generation is bound together by common burdens and opportunities. They endured serious pressure to excel at rote-learning throughout their secondary and college education. As they find their way in the robust modern economy, those with the best credentials have great chances to try a wide variety of positions and job descriptions. There is room for them to pursue entrepreneurial business endeavors or to devote their daily lives to growing Chinese multinational companies. It's characteristic for the 80s generation to work long hours and respect traditional protocol for obedience in the work place. Those who want to advance their professional careers at a faster rate to higher levels will benefit from training that stimulates their creative problem solving skills and nurtures their confidence in taking innovative approaches towards career development. Those who proactively attain the credentials needed to advance to higher levels of industry, by saving and investing in advanced training, will be prepared to take new job opportunities when they are presented to them. In this way, they may make their dreams into reality, support their families, and infuse resiliency throughout the Chinese economy.

Rory Byrne Zimmerman works in Beijing. She is grateful to her friends and colleagues whose opinions and personal experiences contributed greatly to this article.

Visualizing China in Transformation: The Underground and Independent Films of Jia Zhangke

Shu-chin Wu
Vol.9, No.2
2010

In China, Jia Zhangke's films, like other underground (dixia) and independent (duli) films, are more accessible in the little-known film clubs in big cities like Beijing and the living rooms of film critics and scholars than in movie theaters. Although underground and independent are terms fraught with problems and contradictions, here they are used to indicate the non-mainstream, alternative films made in contemporary China that are produced outside the state censorship and studio system and films that contain alternative trends and aesthetics[1]. Among Jia's six feature films that are now available in the United States, three were blocked from domestic screening in China by the state censors. Outside of China, the reception and impact of Jia's films are very different. Jia has attracted attention at international film festivals in Venice, Cannes, Tokyo, and New York. His first "underground" feature film, Xiao Wu (aka The Pickpocket, 1997), after winning a top prize at the 1997 Berlin Film festival, was shown in four French theaters and reportedly topped the French box office for four weeks[2]. Martin Scorsese liked the style of this film so much that he praised Jia for "reinventing

---

1   *For a critical examination of the contradictions and problems in the terms "underground" and "independent," see Paul G. Pickowicz and Yingin Zhang (ed), From Underground to Independent: Alternative Film Culture in Contemporary China (Lanham: Rowan & Littlefield, 2006).*

2   *Yingjin Zhang, "My Camera Doesn't Lie? Truth, Subjectivity, and Audience in Chinese Independent Film and Video" in Paul G. Pickowicz and Yingjin Zhang (eds.), From Underground to Independent: Alternative Film Culture in Contemporary China (Lanham: Rowan & Littlefield, 2006), pp. 37-38.*

cinema."[3] Jia's "above-the-ground" independent feature film Still Life (2006) won the prestigious Golden Lion award at the Venice Film Festival. Jia has been wooed by foreign critics and scholars and is regarded by them as one of the most original and talented contemporary Chinese filmmakers. Dudley Andrew calls Jia "a poet of cinema," while Jonathan Rosenbaum compares Jia to the Hungarian filmmaker Miklos Jancso, and Stephen Teo invokes Raul Ruiz to explain the quality of Jia's films. On March 5, 2010, the Museum of Modern Art in New York began a full retrospective of Jia's films, making Jia the first Chinese filmmaker to have an exhibit in the Museum of Modern Art in more than 20 years.

While some underground and independent Chinese films acquire their popularity abroad by being openly subversive of China's state authority, the films of Jia Zhangke are of a different nature. Even though Jia's films are politically very significant, he does not posit himself as a dissident opposing the Chinese state. Nor does he center his films on political criticism. His films aim to reach beyond ordinary politics and portray the encompassing reality of Chinese people and society[4]. Jia also is not interested in melodramatic treatment of historical traumas and national allegories, as are his predecessors Zhang Yimou and Chen Kaige, two Fifth-generation filmmakers who made Chinese films known overseas in the 1980s by centering on these themes. Viewing the films of Zhang Yimou, Chen Kaige, and others prompted Jia to make films because, he said, "I still haven't seen a single Chinese film that had anything to do with the Chinese reality that I knew."[5]

The reality that Jia knew is the massive transformation--rapid social changes, economic forces, and cultural shifts-that resulted from the Open Door policy and the Four Modernizations initiated by Deng Xiaoping in the 1980s. All of Jia's films illustrate this great transformation that China is going through in the "here and now" (dangxia), with its internal contradictions and its victims-underclass, rural, marginal people (xiao renwu) who not only do not benefit from the promise and hope of the sweeping economic and societal development but have become alienated from and lost in it.

Two films of Jia Zhangke that best capture the power, ironies, problems, and contradictions embedded in China's economic reform and social transformation are Platform (Zhantai, 2000) and Still Life (Shanxia haoren, 2006). Platform, considered as Jia's most ambitious film, is set in the director's birthplace, Feng-

---

3   Michael Berry, *Xiao Wu, Platform, Unknown Pleasures: Jia Zhangke's 'Hometown Trilogy,'* (London: Palgrave MacMillan, 2009), p.8.

4   Scholars have different opinions about the "political" question in China's underground and independent films. The question of the "political" is unsettled mainly because of different conceptions of politics. This question is mentioned in the "Preface" in From Underground to Independent.

5   "In Conversation with Jia Zhangke," in Michael Berry, *Speaking in Images* (New York: Columbia University, 2005).

yang, a small hinterland city in the poverty-stricken Shanxi province in northern China. The narrative of Platform traces the evolution of the lives of members of a "performing arts troupe" (wengongtuan) as they experience and negotiate the difficult and constantly changing reality under Deng's market reforms. The protagonists are two couples; all four of them are members of the performing arts troupe. They are young and idealistic. As the performing arts troupe changes from a government sponsored work unit to a private band, their idealism is confronted with the cruelty of reality. One couple suddenly breaks up as the other couple goes through long estrangement until a final union at the end of the film. It is important to note that Jia's interest is not so much in the plot development of the characters. Rather, he is interested in the subtle human effects of economic and social change.

In the opening scene, we see a group of people in the theater waiting to see the play "The Last Train to Shaoshan," being put on by the performing arts troupe. In the background is a big diagram labeled "Diagram for New Rural Development." It is 1979, shortly after Deng Xiaoping achieved political dominance and announced the new economic policies in the Third Plenum in December 1978. The opening scene signifies change. The members of the performing arts troupe are low-status, young, rural cultural people who work for a government-sponsored cultural unit. The "new rural development" introduced capitalist economics to China's countryside and left groups like the film's performing arts troupe without any choice but to become privatized. It is ironic that the train, a symbol of industrialization, prosperity, and China's future, is only heading for Shaoshan in the fictional play. Shaoshan is Chairman Mao Zedong's birthplace and one of the holy places in socialist China. For the characters of Platform, living under Deng's market reforms, the destination of the symbolic train is not socialism but a peculiar kind of capitalism called "socialism with Chinese characteristics," whose nature is dynamic and unruly and whose social consequences are unpredictable and somehow unsettling.

In the span of 12 years (1979 to 1991, the time during which the film is set), we see China's radical transformation through the transformation of the performing arts troupe. Platform presents a Chinese reality that focuses on the marginal and the quotidian. As Jia expresses, "What I really want to focus on is, over the course of this transformation, who is paying the price? What kinds of people are paying the price?"[6]In this film, through many small, ordinary moments, we see the members of the performing arts troupe as marginal people who struggle in the increasingly commercialized rural economy. They are cultural workers who are not very skilled or clever and who live in Fengyang, geographically distant

---

6   Li Xudong, Zhang Yaxuan, & Gu Zheng, Jia Zhangke dianying: Zhanti (The Films of Jia Zhangke: Platform) (Beijing: Zhongguo mangwen chubanshe, 2003), 191.

from the centers of reform. Their marginality makes them vulnerable in this fast-changing society.

One scene in particular conveys the sorrow and status of their struggle. Toward the end of the film, in a scene set in the middle of the dusty road connecting Fengyang to its neighboring cities, two of the performers dance on the open bed of their transport truck while cars and trucks swiftly pass by. The name of the troupe at this time has been changed from Fengyang County Rural Cultural Work Team to Shenzhen All-stars Rock and Break-dance Electronic Band. The new name reveals the awkwardness of the place in which the troupe finds itself in the new world: their dream of being the stars of Shenzhen, a special economic zone that booms and modernizes under Deng Xiaoping's economic policies, is a stark contrast to their reality. The social results of market reform for the members of the performing arts troupe are a lost past, a fictional present, and an unknown future. They are the people who pay the price during the course of great transformation.

Still Life, like Platform, focuses on the reality of the marginal and the quotidian as it manifests the consequences of China's economic and social transformation. It is set in the ancient town of Fengjie, known for its rich ancient culture and magnificent scenery that inspired beautiful verses from Tang poets Li Bai and Du Fu. Today, Fengjie has also become known as a site of China's controversial Three Gorges Dam project, one of the largest man-made projects in human history, and one that has caused immense human destruction, including the relocation of 1.4 million people as well as large-scale ecological destruction. Jia Zhangke estimates that by the time the shooting of Still Life began in 2005, two-thirds of Fengjie, with many of its archeological and historic sites, had been submerged under water.

It is characteristic of Jia Zhangke not to dwell on the controversial subject of the Three Gorges Dam. Instead, he uses ordinary, rural, marginal people (xiao renwu) and their everyday lives to represent the reality of Fengjie. In contrast to the Chinese state's claim that the Three Gorges Dam is a great social and economic success, what Still Life directs viewers to see in the film is ruins upon ruins. This prompted the famous film scholar and critic Cui Weipin to declare that ruins are the real protagonist in the film.[7]

Ruin is a recurring motif in Jia's films. In Still Life, ruin has a multilayer of meanings. Jia uses the journey of the protagonist Han Sanming, a migrant worker who left his coal-mining job in Shanxi to become a demolition worker in Fengjie to search for his runaway wife whom he purchased illegally 16 years earlier, to illustrate the meanings of ruin. First, Han's demolition job leads us to witness physical ruin everywhere: demolished factories and buildings, abandoned houses,

7   *"Sanxia haoren: guli, bianqian yu Jia Zhangke de xianshi zhuyi"* (Still Life: home, change, and Jia Zhangke's realism) in Ouyang Jianghe ed., *Zhongguo duli dianying fangtan lu* (On the Edge: Chinese Independent Cinema) (Hong Kong: Oxford University Press, 2007), 245.

concrete blocks, broken bricks, and scrap metal. There also is the ruin of communities. Fengjie is a lost community: the house of Han's ex-wife under water, like the houses of many others in Fengjie, and, as a result, she has to leave town and work as a bonded slave on a boat. A group of demolition workers also decides to leave town because they are paid only RMB 50-60 a day for demolition jobs in Fengjie, while coal miners in Shanxi are paid RMB 200 a day. Nature, too, is ruined. A powerful scene illustrates the ruins of nature when Han lifts up a RMB 10 bill and compares the printed picture of Kuimen on it against the actual renowned landscape. The water on the actual landscape is significantly higher than the picture on the RMB 10 bill!

In Jia's films, China's market reforms and its grand state projects such as the Three Gorges Dam have affected the marginal, powerless rural people and their everyday lives. The troupe's traveling and changing status in Platform and Han Sanming's journey to Fengjie in Still Life can be seen as metaphors for China in transformation. The social and cultural consequences of this transformation are ruins everywhere: ruins of nature, ruins of human habitations, ruins of communities and relationships. Jia uses predominately non-professional actors, naturalistic filming environments, long takes, wide-angle compositions, and synchronized recording without noise filtering to depict the ordinary, powerless rural people who are left behind by China's economic development. To borrow from Colin MacCabe's discussion of realism, Jia's visual depiction of China's reality is not just a rendering of reality but the rendering of a reality that is made more real by the use of aesthetic device.[8] The true merit of Jia's films, even more than the use of aesthetic device, is his genuine, humanistic concern and affection for his characters: the xiao renwu of China. His love for his characters is the essence of his films and the source of his art, and it is what makes him the poet of China's underground and independent cinema.[9]

Shu-chin Wu, Ph.D. is associate professor of history at Agnes Scott College, Atlanta, Georgia.

---

8   Colin MacCabe, "Theory and Film: Principles of Realism and Pleasure," Screen 17 (3), 1976, 79-92.

9   Dudley Andrew calls Jia the cinema of poet and Jonathan Rosenbaum calls him a poetic prophet.

China's Higher Education Reform

Guo-hua Wang
Vol. 9, No. 1
2010

Education reform in China has reached a new and crucial stage. The driving force is the need to produce an increasingly knowledgeable workforce equipped to handle the challenges of an economy that is not only growing extremely rapidly, but also becoming increasingly diversified and sophisticated.

The latest reforms are outlined in a comprehensive plan formally called "State Guidelines for Medium-to-Long-Term Education Reform and Development Plan between 2010 and 2020," otherwise known as the Development Plan.[1] A second round of national discussion of the Development Plan has just been completed, and more than 30,000 suggestions were collected, reflecting national involvement in such an important issue. This plan is enormous and comprehensive, and is based on studies of various educational models.

The plan has backing from the highest levels. For example, in September of 2009 Premier Wen Jiabao visited five classes in a middle school in Beijing. He had lunch with students, and held a discussion session with teachers. On October 31, 2009, the government named Yuan Guiren as the new minister of education to lead the reform. The Development Plan's scale, depth and detailed specifics clearly demonstrate the government and Party's determination and ambition.

Two aspects for higher education reform are key: a relaxation of central control, and opening up of the college admission process. The Development Plan specifically calls for the government to release central control, give universities au-

---

1   *The plan, "State Guidelines for Medium-to-Long-Term Education Reform and Development Plan," (*国家中长期教育改革和发展规划纲要*), http://www.chinanews.com.cn/edu/ news/2010/02-28/2142843.shtml*

tonomy, and allow presidents and faculty to run their schools. The government's function is to be limited to providing services and funding, and to making general educational policies. Universities will be governed by national higher education laws combined with regulations set up by institutions themselves. Another striking aspect of the reform plan is modification of the college admission process. The Development Plan states that it will change from the "one-exam-decides-all" method to a thorough evaluation of a student as a whole person using multiple tests and factors.

The plan is divided into four sections. Each section covers several chapters and each chapter includes numerous issues. Section One describes the plan's overall strategy. Section Two lays out missions to accomplish and goals to achieve. Section Three outlines the reform of the educational infrastructure. Section Four provides measurements to ensure implementation. Six chapters are devoted to specific measures, which include the following: strengthening the quality of teaching faculty; increasing the government funding of education to 4% of GDP by 2012; completing education laws and regulations; and ensuring every step of the reform meets the laws and regulations. In order to accomplish these missions and goals, the Development Plan encourages educational institutions to design their own reform programs and policies.

The defined missions of the Development Plan for higher education are to greatly improve the overall quality of education; to advance science, technologies and culture; to accelerate China's modernization process; and to make China a great nation with strong higher education. The goals of the reform are to advance teaching and scientific research; promote collaboration between universities and research institutions so as to speed discovery and innovation; enhance the ability to serve society by providing knowledge consultation and by transferring technologies and research results into products; nurture outstanding talent; and to cultivate a group of internationally recognized Chinese universities and a number of top-ranked Chinese universities in the world by the end of 2020. In short, the goal is to make China's higher education internationally competitive.[2]

Establishment of Chinese Universities

To understand just how significant the current reforms are designed to be, a brief review of Chinese educational history is in order. In fact, the formal establishment of a higher education system in China is relatively recent. It is widely accepted that the first modern Chinese university was established in 1895, right after the Sino-Japanese War (1894-95), which shifted the dominant influence in Asia from China to Japan. The national shame of this defeat awakened the empire of the Qing Dynasty, which accepted a proposal of Mr. Sheng Xuanhuai,

---

2   *Ibid.*

a higher official of the dynasty and an industrialist, to empower the government by building up modern universities to educate and nurture talent with modern technologies in addition to classics. Beiyang University (now Tianjin University) was established in the city of the same name in 1895, followed by Qiushi Academy (currently Zhejiang University) in 1897, and Jingshi University (now Beijing University) in 1898. By the time the People's Republic of China was founded, there were 227 higher institutions in China.[3]

The government that took over in 1949 reorganized higher education according to the model of the Soviet Union. Private universities, including those established by missionaries, were folded into the state. Soviet higher education emphasized specialization rather than comprehensiveness, and reflected the new political ideology and desire for economic development. As a result, some specialized subject colleges were established or separated out from some comprehensive universities. This higher education system served the purpose of the government at the time, and trained the first generation of highly needed intellectuals to build the new economy.

As Maoist-inspired political changes swept the country, Chinese higher education went through ups and downs. From 1958 to 1963, it experienced the Great Leap Forward. The number of Chinese universities and colleges was greatly increased from 229 in 1957, to 841 in 1958, to 1,289 in 1960. The "mistake" was corrected in the following years. In 1963, the number of universities was reduced to 407.[4] The Cultural Revolution started in 1966, pitting student Red Guards against teachers, and paralyzing formal education. A generation of students in the subsequent years essentially lost the opportunity to receive higher education. In 1970, the government allowed certain universities to re-open. However, the admission of college students was mainly decided by recommendations from peasants, workers and soldiers"and primarily based on the applicants' political behavior. In 1977, Deng Xiaoping regained political power and eventually became the paramount leader of the country. One of his first decisions was to resume the national examination system for college admissions. Three national examinations were held from 1977 to 1979. About 18 million high school graduates from 1966 to 1977, who were willing and able to take the exams, participated in these historical educational events, and about 880,000 of them were fortunate to become college students.[5] The college students from these three years have played important roles in advancing social and economic development in China as envisioned by Mr. Deng.

3   Hayhoe, Ruth, *China's Universities 1895-1995, a Century of Cultural Conflict.* New York: Garland Publishing, p.75 (1996).
4   Kang, Ouyang, "Higher Education Reform in China," *Policy Futures in Education.* 2(1): 141-149 (2004).
5   Ibid.

Prelude to the Current Higher Education Reform

With the formalization of a regular national college entrance examination system in the 1980s, Chinese higher education was in the process of recovering and adjusting from previous social upheavals. In 1993, as market reforms deepened, the Central Committee of the Chinese Communist Party and the State Council jointly issued a Program for Education Reform that allowed the establishment of private universities. The Program proclaimed that "the State encourages all sectors of society, including enterprises, institutions, public organizations or groups as well as individual citizens, to run higher education institutions in accordance with law and to participate in and support the reform and development of higher education."[6] Under this policy, some new colleges were founded by non-government entities, which symbolized a major change in the Chinese higher education structure, which used to be completely controlled by the central government. Such a move led to a significantly expanded scale of higher education. College enrollment experienced an unprecedented growth. According to 2007 Ministry of Education statistics, "in 1990, less than 4% of the 18-22 age group was enrolled as students in higher education institutions compared to 22% in 2005." [7]

As the number of universities grew, the demand for education quality also increased. For the first time in Chinese education history, the nation implemented university rankings using a set of criteria and standards to assess quality. A major event in the effort to improve the quality of higher education by the Chinese government was Project 211, launched in 1995. One hundred universities were selected to receive special funding to improve their overall performance. Subsequently, in 1998, the Ministry of Education launched another major initiative named Project 985. The first phase of Project 985 aimed to propel 10 Chinese universities to rankings among the best in the world in the 21st century. This program was subsequently expanded, and additional universities were selected. These two government-funded projects and the university ranking system have made a significant impact on the quality of China's rapidly proliferating institutions of higher education.

In 2001, China was officially admitted to the World Trade Organization, which provided a great arena for exchanges with many other countries leading to opportunities to integrate Chinese education with the world. For example, the Ministry of Education has dispatched many presidents and party secretaries of top-ranked universities to visit and study in developed countries such as the United States and Great Britain. To promote multidisciplinary, academic collabo-

---

6   Yang, Zhong, *"Globalization and Higher Education Reform in China" http://www.aare.edu. au/05pap/zho05780.pdf*

7   Brandenburg, Uwe and Zhu, Jiani, *Higher Education in China in the Light of Massification and Demographic Change: Lessons to be Learned for Germany. Gutersloh: CHE, p. 21 (2007).*

rations, in early 2000 many old Soviet-style subject colleges were combined into comprehensive universities along the lines of large American universities.

Another important change in China's higher education was the 1999 Higher Education Law. It stipulated that "universities are independent legal entities under democratic management."[8] However, as Lin Jianhua, vice president of Beijing University, pointed out: "Current law gives considerable autonomy to Chinese universities, but their rights have been vaguely defined."[9] Together, these developments during the past 20 years have set the stage for the current movement to reform the Chinese education system.

Future Prospects

In order to further reform Chinese education and stimulate economic development in the next decade, Premier Wen Jiabao chaired an Executive Committee that was formed to draft an education development plan in 2008. That committee produced the current reform plan. It is a grand plan that reflects a balance of interests and influences of various groups. By its very nature, education reform inevitably affects wide areas of society. Xu Zhihong, Deputy Chairman of the National People's Congress, pointed out that "as the reform goes deeper and deeper, we will find a lot of fundamental difficulties."[10] Premier Wen echoed that sentiment when he said "We are now facing a lot of dilemmas."[11] One concern is that autonomy for institutions of higher education "will go hand in hand with losing crucial connections " and influence " with powerful government departments."[12] While the plan encourages nurturing students' creativity and independent thinking to foster scientific innovation, it certainly collides with cultural values that cherish obedience as a virtue. Such a cultural collision can only be resolved with time and collective efforts.

Ethical issues go hand in hand with education reform. A big concern among ordinary people arises from the reform of the GaoKao, or national college entrance examination. With GaoKao no longer the only criterion for admission, various other factors such as teacher recommendations and extracurricular activities will enter the picture. Because of these changes, people are worried that new kinds of bribery and corruption will emerge. It is essential that relevant laws be established and enforced. Ethical education should be part of the reform plan. Ultimately, the success of higher education reform will be inextricably intertwined

---

8 Feng, Jianhua, *"Calls for University Reform," Beijing Review* April 9, 2009.
9 *Ibid.*
10 Xu Zhihong *"Talks about Higher Education Issues" China.com.cn http://www.china.org.cn/ china/NPC_CPPCC_2010/2010-03/10/content_19572188.htm*
11 *Ibid.*
12 Cyranoski, David, *"China Debates University Reform," Nature*, 464 (2010) *http://www. nature.com/news/2010/100316/full/464336a.html*

not just with the political and culture development of the society, but also with its ethical evolution.

Guo-hua Wang is the East Asian Studies Librarian at the Woodruff Libraries at Emory University, Atlanta, Georgia.

Differences in Willingness to Express One's Opinion in US and Chinese Online Consumer Interactions

Wei Cai and Leigh Anne Liu
Vol. 9, No. 2
2010

As a unique type of virtual communication, customer-to-customer interaction on the Web has been considered more effective in influencing consumer purchasing behavior than advertising or personal selling. Researchers recognize that by participating in online communication, customers share information and in so doing influence other people's decisions and help others reduce purchase risks. However, a number of studies have found that the flow of information typical for this activity is often characterized by an asymmetry of activity in which a small group of very active participants contribute and a large group of silent participants read others' postings but contribute nothing to the community. There are clear differences in willingness to display opinions in a virtual public.

Degrees of willingness to communicate vary from culture to culture, even in online customer interactions involving the same product. The communication literature suggests that members of different cultures have different communication predispositions and preferences based on how they utilize context as a source of information.

In general, western cultures, in which individualism is highly valued and members are taught to vocalize their desires, privilege personal over collective goals. People from these cultures tend to utilize low-context communication through which "the mass of the information is vested in the explicit code." A low-context culture favors a communication style in which information is incorporated into the message and detailed background is provided in the course of interactions. Said simply, people within this culture are more likely to be explicit, direct, factual, and provide sufficient evidence. On the other hand, Asian cultures, greatly influenced by Confucianism and collectivism that emphasize developing and maintaining harmony within interpersonal relationships and society, tend to utilize high-context communication in which "most of the information is either in the physical context or internalized in the person, while very little is in the coded, explicit, transmitted part of the message." In other words, a high-context culture such as the Chinese culture has a communication style in which most of the information is derived from the context, leaving very little information transmitted explicitly. Additionally, in conflict situations, people in high-context cultures tend to use more abstract, indirect and avoiding styles to let others make inferences from the context so that they can protect interpersonal relationships from embarrassment or disagreement.

The above mentioned differences between low-context cultures and high-context cultures in terms of communication style can be used to develop hypotheses about how groups in American culture and Chinese culture differ in their online engagements and to provide the rationale for such differences since, as Rubin (1998) pointed out, culture plays a critical role in shaping individuals' emotional experiences and the ways they express themselves.

Within a low-context culture, people are more likely to be explicit, direct, factual, and provide sufficient evidence, as is the case western cultures (e.g., American culture). In this type of culture, members tend to speak out, expressing positive and negative emotions, and are more likely to show a high level of willingness to deliver sufficient information and support their opinions.

However, in a high-context culture where the underlying values differ from Western cultures, the behaviors and interactional patterns of online discussions are very likely to be different. Chinese culture, for example, has communication styles in which most of the information is shared by people in society, leaving very little information in the explicit transmitted part of the message, as opposed to the low-context Western cultures. Therefore, members in this type of culture prefer to use indirect messages and deliver them in an abstract, implicit manner. By employing this community style, they can preserve others' face and avoid confrontation.

In an effort to gain a better understanding of the impact of culture on the willingness to communicate, we examined online customer interactions regarding Amazon and Taobao products. Amazon and Taobao are among the largest E-commerce trading platforms in the U.S. and China respectively. In addition, they have similar and active online customer-to-customer posting communities. The study investigated potential culturally related differences in online reviews of the same product, Apple Corp.'s iPad, by Amazon and Taobao customers. Linguistic features of online reviews were analyzed by using the Linguistic Inquiry and Word

Count program.

Based on previous research examining communication styles in different cultures, we hypothesize that behavior in relation to the willingness to communicate and the interactional patterns of online discussions is very different between low- and high-context groups. Since Americans from a low-context culture tend to speak out, regardless of positive or negative emotions, and Chinese from a high-context culture are more likely to employ an implicit and avoiding style to communicate, we further predict that American customers will demonstrate a higher level of willingness to deliver sufficient information to support their opinions than their high-context Chinese counterparts. Specially, low-context Americans are expected to be more willing to express their opinions toward iPad, even their critical negative thoughts, compared to Chinese customers. On the contrary, Chinese customers are hypothesized to demonstrate a lower level of willingness to express their opinions toward iPad, and in particular, to express negative thoughts because they are more indirect and more sensitive to interpersonal relationships. From a linguistic perspective, we hypothesize that low-context Americans, driven by the underlying culture of individualism, are more likely to utilize first-person, singular pronouns than high-context Chinese counterparts, who are highly influenced by the philosophy of collectivism, which can be used as further evidence of their greater willingness to speak out during online interactions.

Data Collection

The data for this study are customer reviews for the iPad G found on the Amazon website http://www.amazon.com/Apple-iPad-MB292LL-Tablet-16GB and the Taobao website http://site.taobao.com/1101/site-100256024-0-0-0-up-down-8.htm. The reviews on Taobao were available only in Chinese and were translated into English. Considering the possibility of bias occurring during the translation, the Chinese version was used as a secondary reference.

Next, randomly selected online postings were analyzed using Pennebaker et al.'s (2001) Linguistic Inquiry Word Count (LIWC). The LIWC tracked and counted the number of words fitting the definition of several meaningful dimensions. For example, the number of times a customer wrote us or our was counted and categorized as the customer using social words. Those linguistic categories that resulted in significant differences in willingness to express themselves by American customers and Chinese customers are reported in the data analysis section.

Lastly, the online postings on both the Amazon and the Taotao websites were coded for Applause and Criticism functions in order to gain a greater understanding of the difference between these two groups in terms of the impact of culture on the willingness to express oneself on the Web.

Data Analysis

Apple's iPad has attention in international markets as well as in the United States. Even before its release in China, growing numbers of authentic iPads were distributed in the country through all kinds of channels, including individual on-line retailers, friends, relatives or online American stores. In this regard, American and Chinese users have had a great opportunity to share their experience in using iPad and to comment on such issues as price, features and problems. Accordingly, comments or reviews on iPad by American and Chinese customers were available on both Amazon and Taobao websites. Overall, on these two websites, some customers gave supportive reviews while others displayed negative ones.

In the U.S., 139 customers participated in online reviews, 75 (around 54.0%) of whom wrote very supportive comments with ratings greater than 3 points. Seventeen posted neutral comments that equaled 3 points in ranking, and 47 (roughly 33.7%) expressed a very negative opinion toward iPad by giving ratings lower than 3 points. Conversely, the Chinese data from Taobao have a total of 228 customer reviews, in which 167 (about 73.2%) left very positive reviews with ratings greater than 3 points, 44 (around 19.3%) gave neutral comments that are equal to 3 points, and 17 (roughly 7.5%) provided very critical reviews with ratings lower than 3 points.

On all three levels of ratings, Amazon customers used more first person singular pronouns (e.g., I, me, my) and social words (e.g., we, us) compared to Taobao customers. Interestingly, among 1-point, very negative reviews, Taobao customers used more social words than Amazon customers.

In order to understand the difference in communication by Amazon customers and Taobao customers, all the online postings were coded for two major functions: Applause and Criticism. Representative words associated with these two pragmatic functions were listed as follows:

Applause: Customers give positive comments on iPad in terms of its significance in the history of the tablet PC, style, quality, performance, etc.

- American Amazon: a tremendous leap in the right direction.../ very fast/ impressive/ absolutely gorgeous/ easy/ the least bit sorry to have bought one/ iPad isn't just making history, it's making an impact on the future of media reading on a whole new level.../ delight/ far easier and better to use than I had expected/ web browsing experience/
- Chinese Taobao: epoch-making product/ more powerful hardware specifications bring outstanding performance/ color quality/ although not the first tablet PC, definitely now the number one. It is a stunner.../ performance/ admire the design/ not a bad choice/ stylish/ very portable/ stylish and very attractive/ the future of tablet PC/

The above data of applause function demonstrate that Amazon customers gave credit to iPad because it is "impressive", "superb", "gorgeous", and "a delight" from their personal perspective and experience. In contrast, Chinese Taobao customers approached iPad's advantages mainly from others' points of view because it looks "stylish", "fashionable", "attractive", and was "a stunner." One possible explanation for this finding is that Americans as individualists focused more on whether the product satisfied their own needs. Conversely, Chinese affected by collectivism put their emphasis on whether iPad can bring others' attention or give them "face."

Criticism: Customers express one kind of disapproval usually by pointing out faults or shortcomings of product, displaying emotions about iPad's price, configuration, and other aspects such as screen, apps, performance, and so on.

Criticism on Price: Both American and Chinese customers showed their disappointment with the high price but they approached it in different ways: Americans directly criticized the price without any reservations; Chinese shied away from sharp criticism in depth by using "little bit" or relatively neutral tones.

- American Amazon: overpriced/ price/ How much money do I have to have so I can enjoy this thing.../ nice device, but high price.../ will I get one? Probably, but not at this price.../ Price tag too high for what it does.../ For $600 you can buy a netbook and a Kindle and have WAY more capability.../ price
- Chinese Taobao: It is for a profligate.../ bit expensive/ / without any logic/ if the price is a little bit more affordable for ordinary people, more people would choose to buy it/ it's not affordable

Criticism on Configuration: Both American and Chinese customers criticized the iPad for its configuration. American customers listed clear and detailed factual evidence in order to support their opinions whereas Chinese made similar criticism without providing too many details.

- American Amazon: brainless browsing board/ if Apple manages to put a CPU into this, I'll be the first to buy one.../ Photoshop, no memory card reader means useless for photographers.../ Even if you could, you still would not be able to compress or decompress zip files or transfer any files in or out of the device via USB, there is no USB...
- Chinese Taobao: The configuration is too low/ USB/ hardware.

Criticism of Other features: Both groups made negative comments on other functions, including screen, connections as well as lack of printing support.

- American Amazon: The screen resolution for movies really sucks, you need to see it.../ serious connectivity problems with the iPad, for which there are no fixes.../ iPad only runs a few truly useful applications, the other 300,000 apps are gimmicks of dubious value.../ it's really fantastic for all the reasons everyone else wrote but it doesn't have flash that's the only stupid thing to me.../ one major flaw - no external video for viewing iPad screen or movies.../ iPad is NO replacement for a netbook, in fact, I don't know what it is at all.../ [printing] is a potentially huge flaw, especially for people who want to use the iPad for editing office documents.../ to hold without a case.

- Chinese Taobao: WiFi is not good/ connection/ It doesn't support multiple-task processing/ camera/ compatibility/ to transfer the data or file.

Criticism based on Holistic Negative Feeling:

- American Amazon: Now I am disappointed because my idealist expectations have not been lived up to.../ I bought one, tested for a week and then resold. And guess what: I don't miss it at all.../ Not bad, but seriously limited.../ I'm frustrated with iPad.
- Chinese Taobao: Overall it is not very good because there are so many accessories that you need to purchase additionally.../ what do we do with this iPad? Probably we can only use it until China is as developed as the U.S.

Data in Criticism show that American customers use more factual information collected from their first-hand experience to support their comments, while Chinese customers employed more implicit and conclusions without providing sufficient factual details to back up their negative thoughts. The differences in the use of factual information showed American customers' full engagement while the prevalence of abstract words demonstrated the Chinese customers' detachment especially from negative comments. As we know, American culture endorses individualism and encourages members to express themselves overtly, emphasizing independence from groups by highlighting individual accomplishment and personal goals. So speech acts such as criticizing sharply or refusing directly are acceptable. Conversely, culture is known for its implicit and face-oriented way of communication driven by collectivism. With the purpose of maintaining harmony with others or society, speech acts such as making negative comments or refusals are considered face-threatening, and members often utilize implicitness or abstractness to help mitigate the potential possible damage to interpersonal relationships caused by full confrontation. In addition, research has shown that the degree of context and the amount of information in a culture effectively differentiate the communication styles between communications in Eastern as opposed to Western cultures. High-context Chinese customers are more likely to employ an implicit abstract manner to communicate than their low-context U.S. counterparts.

Discussion

The present study utilized Hall's (1976) concepts of high- and low-context-cultures and major cultural factors identified in previous research, such as individualism-collectivism, to examine how cultural aspects relevant to these two components may influence in willingness to express one's opinion in online interactions by American customers on Amazon and Chinese customers on Taobao about the iPad. As hypothesized, the analysis presented in this article demonstrated that these two groups' willingness to speak out differed in several ways. First, customers appeared to be more direct and more willing to speak out, regardless of positive and negative opinions, whereas Chinese counterparts developed indirect means of communicating, making a greater use of implicit and information. In the Chinese culture, openness and frankness can at times be considered positive, but they can also be viewed as negative, especially when dealing with negative emotions, which explains why Chinese customers expressed themselves in a more avoiding, abstract style. Another aspect of the impact of culture on the willingness to express oneself is the heavy use of first person singular pronouns and references to the self by American customers in the American data, compared with their Chinese counterparts. According to Newman, Pennebaker, Berry, & Richards' notion (2003), the use of the first person singular pronouns is a method of declaring ownership of a statement, which might be explained by the individualist nature of American people in which the self-value is relatively emphasized versus the group or society. American customers emphasize me in order to have their individual accomplishments, thoughts, and abilities recognized by others or society.

Limitations

One limitation of this study is that a convenience sample was used. Another is the sample size. Specifically, the data analysis was solely based on online reviews of one product, iPad. The third limitation rests with the fact that only the impact of cultural dimensions related to low/high contexts and individualism-collectivism were explored in the study. Differences in willingness to speak out by American and Chinese groups might also result from other factors such as individual differences (e.g., age, gender, education, etc.). Thus caution should be exercised in interpreting the findings. The fourth limitation of this study is that a small number of randomly selected reviews were chosen using the Pennebaker et al.'s (2001) LIWC. Ideally, mean differences should be sought by using a large sample. Therefore, the generalization of the results is limited. Finally, online reviews of iPad by Chinese users might have been affected by the fact that the iPad had not been officially released into the Chinese market at the time of this study. However, the study's findings provide directions for future research. Although the assumption that the U.S. and China are considered to be lower and higher context cultures, respectively, has been widely accepted, there are few studies in which this assumption was tested in the context of online reviews. The imitativeness and findings of the present study should be considered valuable in this regard. Additionally, the current study attempted to integrate cross-cultural communication with asymmetric online discussion in a business setting. It would be interesting to see whether the findings also apply to face-to-face communication. In sum, this small-sample study lends support to the validity of the hypotheses proposed, which can be further tested with a well-designed, large sample study in the future.

References

1. Bickart, Barbara & Schindler, Robert M. (2001). "Internet forums as influential sources of consumer information," *Journal of Interactive Marketing, 15(3): 31-40.*

2. Brown, P. & Levinson, S. D. (1987). *Politeness: Some Universals in Language Usage.* Cambridge: Cambridge University Press.

3. Cho, B., Kwon, U., Gentry, J. W., Jun, S. & Kropp, F. (1999). "Cultural values reflected in theme and execution: a comparative study of US and Korean television commercials," *Journal of Advertising, 28(4): 59-73.*

4. Gruen, Thomas W., Osmonbekov, Talai, & Czaplewski, Andrew J. (2006). "eWOM: The impact of customer-to-customer online know-how exchange on customer value and loyalty," *Journal of Business Research, 59(4): 449-456.*

5. Hall, E. T. (1976). *Beyond Culture. New York: Doubleday.*

6. Jiang, X. G. (2006). "Cross-cultural pragmatic differences in US and Chinese press conferences: the case of the North Korea nuclear crisis," *Discourse Analysis. 17(2): 237-257.*

7. Kim, D., Pan, Y. & Part, H. (1998). "High- versus low-context culture: a comparison of Chinese, Korean, and American cultures," *Psychology and Marketing, 15: 507-521.*

8. Merkin, Rebecca S. (2009). "Cross-cultural communication patterns - Korean and American communication," *Journal of Intercultural Communication, Retrieved from http://www.immi.se/intercultural/nr20/merkin.htm*

9. Newman, M. L., Pennebaker, J. W., Berr, D. S., & Richards, J. M. (2003). "Lying words: Predicting deception from linguistic styles," *Personality and Social Psychology Bulletin, 29: 664-675.*

10. Pennebaker, J. W., Francis, M. E., & Booth, R. J. (2001). *Linguistic inquiry and word count. Mahwah, NJ: Lawrence Erlbaum.*

11. Pollach, I. (2008). "Media richness in online consumer interactions: An exploratory study of consumer-opinion web sites," *Information Resources Management Journal, 21(4): 49-65.*

12. Rafaeli, S., Ravid, G., & Soroka, V. (2004). "De-lurking in virtual communities: A social communication network approach to measuring the effects of social and cultural capital," *Paper presented at the 37th International Conference on System Sciences, Big Island, Hawaii.*

13. Rubin, K. H. (1998). "Social and Emotional Development from a Cultural Perspective," *Developmental Psychology, 34(4): 611-615.*

14. Shen, F., Wang, N., Guo, S., & Guo, L. (2009). "Online network size, efficacy, and opinion expression: Assessing the impacts of internet use in China," *International Journal of Public Opinion Research, 21(4): 451- 476.*

15. Ting-Toomey, S., Yee-Yung, K., Shapiro, R., Garcia, W., Wright, T., & Oetzel, J. (2000). "Ethnic/cultural identity salience and conflict styles in four U.S. ethnic groups," *International Journal of Intercultural Relationships, 24: 47-82.*

Wei Cai earned her MBA degree at the Robinson College of Business at Georgia State University, Atlanta, Georgia. Leigh Anne Li, Ph.D. is an associate professor of international business at Georgia State University.

China 2030: An Analysis of the World Bank's Reform Strategy

Zhenhui Xu
Vol.11, No.1
2012

China has achieved remarkable economic success since Deng Xiaoping initiated economic reforms in the late 1970s. For more than three decades, China's GDP growth rate averaged 10% per year, accompanied by drastic declines in poverty rates, rising sophistication in manufacturing, improvement in infrastructure and the re-inventing of enterprises into globally competitive companies. The question now is how China can move to the next stage of development and continue to grow. In its 2012 report, "China 2030: Building a Modern, Harmonious, and Creative High-Income Society," the World Bank, in cooperation with a high-level Chinese research team, systematically reviewed the country's successes and coming challenges and recommended further reforms for lifting the Chinese economy to a higher level.

A key aspect of China's success has been the opening of the domestic economy to international trade and investment while promoting exports. According to the World Bank's World Development Indicators 2011, the value of China's exports in 1978 was US$9.8 billion while imports amounted to US$10.5 billion, accounting for less than 0.6% of the world's total. By the end of 2010, however, Chinese exports reached US$1.58 trillion, 161 times higher than in 1978, while the value of imports reached US$1.40 trillion, 133 times the 1978 figure. Today China is the world's largest exporter (accounting for 10% of the world's total) and second-largest importer (accounting for 9% of the world's total). This dramatic increase in trade has helped the Chinese economy become the second largest in the world, trailing only the U.S.

But heavy reliance on exports for economic growth may not be sustainable in the long run, especially for a country as large as China. In the recent global economic crisis, numerous factories and companies in China shut down. Unemployment rose, particularly in the coastal region where most of China's exports were manufactured. Weakness abroad dragged China's economic growth to its lowest level in years. In November 2008, the Chinese central government launched a 4-trillion-yuan (approximately US$586 billion) stimulus plan, one goal of which was increasing domestic demand and expanding internal markets. This decision represented an important shift in China's development strategy.

In its report, the World Bank suggests that China is near an inflection point of its economic growth and offers six recommendations to move the country forward. They are: strengthening the foundations for a market-based economy, fostering innovation, going "green," expanding and promoting social security for all, improving the fiscal system and seeking mutually beneficial relations with the world. According to Reuters, at the launch of "China 2030" in Beijing on February 27, 2012, World Bank President Robert Zoellick was blunt, saying, "As China's leaders know, the country's current growth model is unsustainable." He urged China to get ahead of events and adapt to major changes in the Chinese and world economies.

The World Bank report has been the subject of intense debate within China. As with policy changes anywhere, winners and losers will emerge if the recommendations are implemented. Therefore, further reforms will depend on their political feasibility.

China must face many tough issues immediately as well as down the road in order to foster sustainable growth. For example, urbanization has been and will continue to be a gigantic challenge. China's urban population exceeded 50% of the country for the first time at the end of 2011, and is expected to reach 70% by 2030 (China Daily, April 4, 2012). The CIA estimates that China's rate of urbanization between 2010 and 2015 will be 2.3% per year. And with rapid urbanization comes ever-growing construction. High-rise residential buildings are mushrooming in China's cities. Yet urbanization requires more than housing. In an interview with Xinhua News Agency, Zheng Xinli, vice-chairman of the China Center for International Economic Exchange, points out that each additional percentage-point increase in urban population means more than 10 million rural residents becoming city dwellers — and each new arrival requires at least 100,000 yuan (US$15,873) in infrastructure investment. Huge migration and rapid urbanization will undoubtedly pose great challenges, not only for infrastructure but also for the environment, social security and government budgets. Yet in his speech at the 2012 annual meeting of the Boao Forum for Asia (BFA) in China's Hainan Province, Robert Zoellick said if carried out properly, urbanization could be the foundation of China's future growth.

At the opening of the annual meeting of the 11th National People's Congress on March 5, 2012, Chinese Premier Wen Jiabao announced that China's GDP growth will slow to 7.5% in 2012. This target is the lowest in more than 30 years. The aim is to allow China to adjust macroeconomic structures and promote quality growth instead of speedy growth for its own sake.

The Chinese are fully aware that they are facing major issues with energy use and pollution. World Bank data show that China's energy use per capita (in kilograms of oil equivalent) was 618 kg in 1978 but reached 1,695 kg in 2009. According to the Worldwatch Institute's Worldwatch Report (2011), however, China has prioritized green development in almost all leading economic sectors in the past decade, especially during the 11th five-year period of 2006-2010. With the enactment of a landmark renewable energy law in 2005, China made the development of renewable energy a national priority. By 2007, the country had the world's largest number of hydroelectric generators and was obtaining 8% of its energy and 17% of its electricity from renewable sources. In China's western region where wind, sunshine and other natural resources are abundant, sizable windmill farms have been built, solar hot-water heaters are the norm in households and taxi cabs run on natural gas rather than gasoline. China has made important progress in the area of renewable energy.

Another critical area of reform relates to the role of government. Government interference is highest in China's financial sector, which has been monopolized by a few large banks with severe barriers to private capital. In addition, bank loans to local governments for development and construction pose potential threats to China's financial stability. Although China is one of the world's largest creditor nations, local governments have accumulated worrisome amounts of debt, and some already are having difficulty paying it back.

So far, the Chinese currency, the renminbi (RMB), still is not convertible. But it is in China's interest to fulfill its global responsibilities and make the RMB a convertible currency as soon as it can. The People's Bank of China (China's central bank) recently proposed an acceleration of capital controls aimed at making the RMB a global reserve currency (People's Daily, February 23, 2012). In a statement published on its website on April 14, 2012, the People's Bank announced that the daily floating band for the RMB in the inter-bank foreign exchange spot market would be expanded from the previous 0.5% to 1% effective April 16. Premier Wen Jiabao, meanwhile, told reporters that the Chinese central government had unified its thinking and decided to break the monopoly of a few large banks and allow private capital to enter China's financial sector (Southern Metropolitan Daily, April 4, 2012). He further said that financial reforms piloted in Wenzhou would be implemented across the country, some of them immediately.

Still, the World Bank's recommendations by no means will be easily put in place or accepted without challenge. Strengthening the foundations for a market-based economy has set off particular disagreement and debate. At a press conference during the launch of "China 2030" in Beijing, an angry Chinese demonstrator, Du Jianguo, interrupted World Bank President Zoellick's speech on privatizing state-owned enterprises (SOEs) by storming onto the podium, handing out pamphlets and yelling that the World Bank is poisoning China. Du claimed to be an "independent" scholar, i.e. not affiliated with any Chinese institution or organization. But he is not alone; many Chinese, including government officials, oppose the World Bank's report.

At the press conference, Zoellick revealed that the project to study China's economic challenges was initiated 18 months earlier with the support of Vice Premier Li Keqiang. The project was done under the authority of China's Ministry of Finance, with the cooperation of the Development Research Center of the State Council (DRC), a top think-tank that advises China's cabinet. According to a behind-the-scenes account that has been reported in China (http://business.sohu.com/20120229/n336252696.shtml), the Finance Ministry sent the draft report to all relevant ministries and agencies for comment. The Ministry of Education and Ministry of Health praised the document, saying that it provided productive recommendations for further reforms and development in China's education and health care system. But the State-owned Assets Supervision and Administration Commission of the State Council (SASAC) strongly opposed it, claiming the recommendation to privatize SOEs and reduce the profile of SOEs in the Chinese economy was unconstitutional. The commission offered to debate the question with the World Bank and the DRC. Resulting negotiations between the SASAC and and DRC produced a softened final report.

Advantages afforded to SOEs long have been a source of controversy. Critics have argued that undue government protection has given state enterprises market power and easy access to bank loans and other financial resources, shielding them from competition. Despite their shrinking share in the economy, SOEs still play an important role. According to the Second National Economic Census (2008), assets held by SOEs accounted for about 30% of the 208 trillion RMB in total assets of industrial and service-sector companies, while the number of SOEs accounted for only 3.1% of total enterprises. These numbers suggest that the average size of SOEs is much greater than that of non-SOEs.

Employment is an important social function for SOEs. State enterprises still are a vital source of jobs in China even though their share of total urban employment has been shrinking. When economic reforms were just starting in 1980, SOEs employed 76% of China's urban workers, while urban collectively owned enterprises (UCOEs) employed the remainder. In 2000, only 35% of China's urban workers were employed by SOEs. Their share was further reduced to 19% in 2010 when they employed more than 65 million urban workers. Despite this reduction, in some areas SOEs are China's most important employers. For example, a total of 58,000 new urban workers were added in Qinghai Province in 2010. Almost one-fourth, or 14,900 workers, were hired by SOEs.

China is known to have abundant labor, but economic growth in the past three decades has pushed labor costs up. The "population dividend" is gradually disappearing, hurting China's SOEs the most. Private companies in China have reacted to rising labor costs by mechanizing, innovating and moving out of the higher-cost coastal areas to the lower-cost interior. Some foreign companies have even pulled out of China entirely. Yet there is not much evidence that China's SOEs have adopted similar strategies. SOEs still provide a significant percentage of urban Chinese workers with employment, social security and health care that underpins access to a decent life. The impact of SOEs on the Chinese economy cannot be underestimated. The debate about how to reform China's state enterprises will surely be contentious.

The World Bank's report stops short of being overly prescriptive, as it is a joint product between the World Bank and the DRC of the State Council. But the implication of its broad recommendations is easy to see. Although it does not say so explicitly, some recommendations clearly require political and social reforms as well. Therefore, the participation of the DRC is significant. With a semi-official stamp of approval, reformers in China can better prepare to move forward, and, as noted earlier, some changes already have started.

For obvious reasons, the Chinese government must balance what is economically superior with what is politically and socially practical. Economic growth through heavy investment and cheap labor alone is not sustainable in the long run because diminishing returns will eventually kick in. Therefore, the importance of establishing a sound economic system is self-evident. Without much-needed reforms in the six vital areas, it will be very difficult, if not impossible, for China to improve its overall economic efficiency. The Chinese government and public eventually will have to make tough choices concerning the issues outlined in the World Bank's report. The question is, after decades of reforms initiated by Deng Xiaoping, how China will move forward.

Zhenhui X, Ph.D. is professor of economics at Georgia College and State University, Milledgeville, Georgia.

China's Response to U.S. Pressure to Revalue the RMB

Lee Taylor Buckley
Vol.11, No.1
2012

Introduction

As the U.S. presidential election draws nearer and the People's Republic of China also faces a year of leadership change, the issue of Chinese currency revaluation has garnered an increasing amount of attention in both countries. Already, American voters have seen Republican presidential candidate Mitt Romney assert that the U.S. must take a more aggressive stance in demanding that the renminbi (RMB) appreciate against the U.S. dollar. RMB appreciation would make Chinese goods more expensive for U.S consumers and U.S. goods less expensive for Chinese consumers, thus increasing U.S. exports and Chinese imports and improving the U.S. trade deficit with China. China, however, has refused to fully satisfy U.S. demands, despite Romney's pledge to declare China a currency manipulator on day one of his presidency should he be elected.[1] Thus, the relevance of the currency revaluation issue cannot be underestimated.

Since Secretary of the Treasury John Snow's visit to China in 2003, the U.S. has persistently pressed Beijing to allow the RMB to appreciate, and China has, in fact, responded positively, allowing the RMB to appreciate by 40 percent over 7 years, from the time China adopted a floating exchange rate in July 2005 to February 2012.[2] At the same time, using the People's Bank of China (PBC) and the official Xinhua news agency, Beijing has advanced a set of arguments against rapid RMB appreciation. Beijing apparently hopes that principled refutation of

---

1   John Harwood, *"The Electoral Math of Romney's Stance on Trade with China,"* 22 March 2012, *The New York Times website.* http://www.nytimes.com/2012/03/23/us/politics/mitt-romneys-stance-on-china-trade.html?pagewanted=all

2   David Leonhardt, *"As China's Currency Rises, U.S. Keeps Up Its Pressure,"* 15 February 2012, *The New York Times website.* http://www.nytimes.com/2012/02/16/business/global/appreciation-in-chinas-currency-goes-largely-unnoted.html

U.S. demands coupled with slow, incremental compliance will placate the U.S. Congress and Treasury Department and foster stable relations between the two countries. This two-pronged response arises from China's important yet conflicting policy objectives. On the one hand, the People's Bank of China, the country's central bank, has affirmed that a policy of incremental appreciation is needed to maintain the country's economic stability and encourage economic growth. On the other hand, China argues that appreciating the RMB against the U.S. dollar too quickly will disrupt the developing country's export-led economy, potentially resulting in instability in the form of unemployment, mass migration and labor strikes. The combination of incremental RMB appreciation with arguments against U.S. pressure can be explained partly by a rational government strategy for maintaining stability and partly by a perceived need to project an image of an independent China that does not capitulate to foreign demands. Ultimately, however, both U.S. pressure and China's own goals to rebalance its export-dependent economy call for further currency appreciation, and therefore it is likely that China will continue to appreciate the RMB.

Factors Pushing China toward RMB Appreciation

The main factor pushing China toward RMB appreciation is U.S. pressure, considering that China does not wish to jeopardize the stability resulting from lucrative trade with the U.S. This point is demonstrated by the fact that China has appreciated the RMB only when the U.S. has threatened punitive measures otherwise. For instance, on July 21, 2005, the People's Bank of China implemented a managed floating exchange rate regime, which resulted in a 2.1% appreciation of the RMB.[3] In February of that year, Senators Charles Schumer and Lindsey Graham introduced a bill demanding China "make a good faith effort to revalue its currency upward placing it at or near its fair market value" within 180 days or risk a 27.5% tariff on any article it exported to the U.S.[4] The second time China appreciated the RMB was on May 21, 2007, when the People's Bank widened the trading band in which the RMB could float against the U.S. dollar from 0.3% to 0.5% in daily movement.[5] This followed renewed threats of a vote on the 27.5% tariff bill. Sen. Schumer ominously stated, "We are not satisfied with simply a 2% revaluation," and under this persistent threat of U.S. tariffs, China again responded by allowing the RMB to appreciate.[6] By July 2008, the RMB had appreciated

---

3   David Barboza, *"Revaluation's Effect on China Travel," 7 August 2005, The New York Times website. http://www.nytimes.com/2005/08/07/travel/07advyuan.html*

4   *109th Congress Bill Text S.295.IS, 3 Feb. 2005, Senate and House of Representatives of the United States of America, Library of Congress website. http://thomas.loc.gov/cgi-bin/query/ z?c109:S.295:*

5   *Zhu Qiwen and Xin Zhiming, "Exchange Rate Could Float in Wider Band," 26 May 2007, China Daily website. http://www.chinadaily.com.cn/china/2007-05/26/content_880766.htm*

6   *Anjali Athavaley, "Schumer and Graham May Press for China Tariffs," 29 July 2005,*

21% against the dollar.[7]

There is evidence that China might not have appreciated the RMB of its own accord. From mid-July 2008 to mid-June 2010, the RMB exchange rate began to plateau at around 6.83 yuan to the dollar.[8] With the onset of the global financial crisis in 2008, China started to experience an economic slump caused by decreased demand for Chinese goods. It appears that the Chinese government did not want to aggravate the ailing condition of the export industry by continuing to allow the yuan to appreciate. Schumer, however, and 13 other senators introduced a bill in March 2010 requiring the U.S. Secretary of the Treasury to provide Congress with biannual reports identifying any country found to have a "fundamentally misaligned currency" and requiring the Commerce Department to impose tariffs on specified goods from those countries.[9] China was a primary target, but Treasury Secretary Timothy Geithner chose to delay the report in April 2010, leaving an enduring threat of potential tariffs against China. As a result, on June 19, 2010, the People's Bank announced it had "decided to proceed further with reform of the RMB exchange rate regime and to enhance the RMB exchange rate flexibility."[10] The Chinese currency appreciated by roughly another 3% against the U.S. dollar from June 19 to October 15, when the U.S. Treasury Department announced that it would again delay the publication of the report on international exchange rate policies, citing China's progress.[11] Slight appreciation would not satisfy the U.S. for long, however, and finally, in October 2011, the Senate passed the Currency Exchange Rate Oversight Reform Act by a vote of 63-35. While it remains uncertain how the bill might fare in the House of Representatives, passage in the Senate is the closest the U.S. government has come to retaliating against China's currency undervaluation, and it has led the Chinese government to lobby Congress against further action. As of April 16, 2012, China also has allowed as much as 1% in daily fluctuation of RMB value, up from the 0.5% limit set in May 2007.[12] Clearly, China has not ignored pressure from the

---

Washington Post website http://www.washingtonpost.com/wp-dyn/content/article/2005/07/28/AR2005072802040.html

7   Daniel Ikenson, "Chinese Currency Rise Will Have a Negligible Effect on the Trade Deficit," 24 March 2010, Cato Institute website. http://www.cato.org/pubs/ftb/FTB-041.pdf

8   Wayne M. Morrison and Marc Labonte, "China's Currency: An Analysis of the Economic Issues," 3 August 2011, Congressional Research Service, Federation of American Scientists website. http://www.fas.org/sgp/crs/row/RS21625.pdf

9   "As Trade Deals Head towards Approval, Backlash Grows against China," 8 October 2011, The Economist website. http://www.economist.com/node/21531486

10   People's Bank of China Statement, "Further Reform the RMB Exchange Rate Regime," 19 June 2010, People's Bank of China website. http://www.pbc.gov.cn/publish/english/955/2010/20100622144059351137121/20100622144059351137121_.html

11   Treasury Department Statement Regarding Decision to Delay the International Economic and Exchange Rate Policies Report to Congress, 15 October 2010, U.S. Department of the Treasury website. http://www.treasury.gov/press-center/press-releases/Pages/tg910.aspx

12   Keith Bradsher, "China Adjusts Currency Trading Rules," 14 April 2012, The New York

U.S. Congress and Treasury Department, but instead enacted policy changes in July 2005, May 2007, June 2010 and April 2012 in response.

China's National Strategy to Gain Time

Naturally, Chinese officials have asserted that policies appreciating the RMB were introduced because they were in China's national interest. The People's Bank of China has stated that its purpose was to "safeguard the overall stability of China's foreign economic and trade environment…as well as the sustained, coordinated and healthy growth of the Chinese economy."[13] Appreciation of the RMB could contribute to future economic growth by making imported products cheaper for Chinese buyers, thereby stimulating domestic demand. However, as China's economy stands today, growth is largely export-led, benefitting from an undervalued currency that makes its exports relatively cheap. The face of the Chinese economy must change before benefiting from RMB appreciation in this way, and for this reason, Chinese officials have listed "the rise in domestic consumption" as a key target of economic restructuring in their 12th Five-Year Plan.[14]

It follows that Chinese policymakers would want to gain time for structural change before enacting exchange rate policy changes. A wider RMB trading band allows the currency to fluctuate nearer fair market value but does not address the U.S. demand that China quickly revalue the currency upward.[15] In fact, the PBC has said that hastening RMB appreciation before enacting reforms in state-owned commercial banks and liberalizing service trades could jeopardize the country's domestic economic stability.[16] Essentially, China claims while exchange rate reform is one element of the overall restructuring effort, it need not be the first.

Another argument intended to buy time for Chinese policymakers suggests that the exchange rate plays an important role in stability during times of crisis – such as the current economic downturn. Keeping the RMB undervalued was helpful in the 1990s, facilitating the accumulation of large foreign reserves that acted as insurance and allowed China to avoid seeking IMF assistance during the Asian Financial Crisis.[17] More recently, Xinhua assured its readers that China is

Times website, *http://www.nytimes.com/2012/04/15/business/global/china-adjusts-currency-trading-rules.html?_r=3&scp=1&sq=China%20curency%20trading%20rules&st=cse*

13   Speech by Zhou Xiaochuan before Inauguration Ceremony of The People's Bank of China Shanghai Head Office, 10 August 2005, The People's Bank of China website. *http://www.pbc.gov.cn/publish/english/956/1943/19432/19432_.html*

14   Deng Shasha, "Key Targets of China's 12th Five-Year Plan," 5 March 2011, Xinhua English News website. *http://news.xinhuanet.com/english2010/china/2011-03/05/c_13762230.htm*

15   Paul R. La Monica, "China and the U.S.: It's Complicated," 16 April 2012, CNN Money website, *http://money.cnn.com/2012/04/16/markets/thebuzz/index.htm*

16   Zhou Xiaochuan, Interview with Xinhua News Agency, "Questions on RMB Exchange Rate," 3 September 2003, The People's Bank of China website. *http://www.pbc.gov.cn/publish/english/955/1983/19839/19839_.html*

17   Aditya Bindal, "Strategic Implications of China's Foreign Exchange Reserves," April 2010,

"sticking to its appreciation policy amid the unfolding global crisis…ensuring the continued growth and stability within its own economy."[18] The U.S., meanwhile, argues that stockpiling foreign reserves aggravates the trade imbalance between the two countries.

China vocally denies that its decisions have been in response to U.S. complaints. Chinese Central Bank Governor Zhou Xiaochuan maintained that in setting exchange rate policy, the PBC would mainly take into consideration the "domestic economic situation and balance of payments rather than the bilateral trade deficits or surpluses with some individual countries."[19] If there were any doubt this statement was directed at the U.S., Zhou also asserted that "the U.S. trade deficit may be attributable to structural imbalances and fiscal deficits in the United States rather than the RMB exchange rate."[20] He went on: China would "push ahead with the reform of the RMB exchange rate regime on a well-planned and step-by-step basis. Relevant policy measures will only be taken at the proper time."[21] Given China's history of exploitation by Western powers over the past 200 years, insisting it will not yield to foreign dictates on RMB appreciation may be a means of saving face. Interestingly, however, "the proper time" has always been directly after the application of U.S. pressure.

Factors Pushing China against RMB Appreciation

A more valuable RMB means China's manufactured goods will be more expensive and thus less competitive in America, its top export destination. The importance of exports to China's economic stability cannot be underestimated. The IMF reports that "fixed investment related to tradable goods plus net exports together accounted for over 60% of China's GDP growth from 2001 to 2008 (up from 40% from 1990 to 2000), which was significantly higher than in the G-7 countries (16%), the euro area (30%) and the rest of Asia (35%)."[22] For a developing country reliant on manufactured exports, RMB appreciation could be detrimental to the stability and growth of China's economy overall.

Disruption of the Chinese economy also affects social stability, which has been

Keck Center for International and Strategic Studies website. http://www.claremontmckenna. edu/keck/student/BindalAFellowshippaper050310.pdf

18   Mo Honge, "Forcing Yuan Appreciation Benefits Nobody," 10 October 2011, Xinhua English News website. http://news.xinhuanet.com/english2010/indepth/2011-10/10/c_131182105. htm

19   Zhou Xiaochuan, Interview with People's Daily, "Exclusive Interview with People's Daily," 8 May 2005, The People's Bank of China website. http://www.pbc.gov.cn/publish/english/956/1942/19425/19425_.html

20   Zhou Xiaochuan, Interview with Xinhua News Agency, "Questions on RMB Exchange Rate," 3 September 2003, The People's Bank of China website. http://www.pbc.gov.cn/publish/english/955/1983/19839/19839_.html

21   Zhou, Interview with People's Daily

22   Morrison and Labonte, "China's Currency: An Analysis of the Economic Issues"

shaken by export-related job issues, including numerous strikes. Chinese officials fear two probable reactions of export producers to appreciation of the RMB: shutting down factories when they can no longer compete, or holding down wages to remain competitive. Either way, unrest can result from loss of jobs as manufacturers are forced out of business, or from worker demonstrations as wages suffer.

Chinese agricultural products also would be less competitive globally with a higher valuation of the RMB. A stronger yuan would facilitate cheaper agricultural imports and cut into profits from agricultural exports. This could result in job and income losses for China's large rural populations, where many are employed in labor-intensive farm jobs. Cities would then feel a further strain as even more people in agricultural areas migrate in search of comparatively fewer jobs in less-labor-intensive sectors. Again, Chinese policymakers opt not to appreciate the RMB quickly in hopes of maintaining economic growth while avoiding unrest.

China's Media and Soft Power

Projecting independence when it comes to exchange rate policy has been a theme in the state-controlled Chinese media. The Xinhua news agency has highlighted the claim that "the yuan exchange rate did not cause the trade imbalance between China and the United States," and that targeting the yuan is no antidote to global economic problems.[23] Saving face also is an obvious goal, as seen in Xinhua's declarations that "the yuan's appreciation will not compromise to foreign pressure, and China will write its own ticket on the pace of its currency's appreciation."[24] Some argue that Xinhua is a way for the Chinese government to exercise soft power by "countering the dominance of Western news outlets and conveying a Chinese perspective on events" within the country and increasingly abroad, through outlets such as CNC World, its global English-language TV channel.[25]

China also has exercised soft power by launching an unprecedented lobbying effort through a Congressional liaison team in the Chinese embassy in Washington. This team reportedly has arranged meetings with key lawmakers' aides and made phone calls to congressional offices in an attempt to kill the Currency Exchange Rate Oversight Reform Act. Through the Foreign Agents Registration Act, it's also known that the Embassy is drawing on the lobbying expertise of Patton

23 Liu Xiao, "Chinese Ambassador Says Stronger Yuan Alone Won't End U.S. Job Woes," 19 November 2011, Xinhua English News website. http://news.xinhuanet.com/english2010/china/2011-11/19/c_131257545.htm

24 Liang Jun, "RMB's Appreciation to Remain Gradual," 13 September 2011, China News website. http://www.china.org.cn/business/2011-09/13/content_23400908.htm

25 Anton Troianovski, "China Agency Nears Times Square," 30 June 2010, The Wall Street Journal Online. online.wsj.com/article/SB10001424052748704334604575339281420753918.html

Boggs, a Washington law firm, at an estimated cost of $35,000 a month.[26]

Though the cost to China could potentially be far higher should the Currency Exchange Rate Oversight Reform Act pass the House of Representatives, Speaker John Boehner has hinted that the chances it will ever be voted on are slim, saying that he considered it "dangerous to be moving legislation through the United States Congress forcing someone to deal with the value of their currency."[27] Nevertheless, the bill's introduction serves as a tangible demonstration of American discontent with Chinese policy. China's response to that discontent likely depends in great part on the Chinese perception of America's motives. Chinese Vice Premier Wu Yi appears to think that the push for "considerable revaluation cannot help at all and could probably injure the interests of the two countries and the public."[28] Why, then, does the Chinese government believe that the U.S. wants it so badly? China may conclude that the real objective is not to bolster the U.S. economy but to repress the Chinese economy. In an exclusive interview with Xinhua, Premier Wen Jiabao said flatly, "the purpose is to hold back China's development."[29] Xinhua added, "China would not yield to foreign pressure for the appreciation of its currency, or renminbi, in any form."[30] Almost two years later, The People's Bank of China announced that the bill passed by the U.S. Senate would not solve its problems, but "might seriously affect the progress of China's reform of the exchange rate regime and might also result in a trade war."[31] Thus, future Sino-U.S. relations are likely to be significantly affected by the Chinese perception of Congressional pressure to appreciate the RMB. If pressure is perceived as an injurious attempt to hold China back, it could be grounds for China to instigate a trade war. Similarly, U.S. election rhetoric also has the potential to influence how China perceives and responds to U.S. pressure in the future. Accordingly, Mitt Romney's threats to declare China a currency manipulator may, in China's view, foreshadow a future trade war, prompting China to pursue a soft power strategy

---

26 Tim Reid and Susan Cornwell, *"China Launches Lobbying Push on Currency Bill,"* 11, Oct. 2011, Reuters website. *http://www.reuters.com/article/2011/10/11/us-usa-china-lobbying-idUSTRE79A76S20111011*

27 Zhang Jun, *"Obama Says Currency Bill on China Could Fall Foul of WTO Rules,"* 7 October 2011, *http://news.xinhuanet.com/english2010/world/2011-10/07/c_131177102.htm*

28 Zhu Qiwen and Xin Zhiming, *"Exchange Rate Could Float in Wider Band,"* 26 May 2007, China Daily website. *http://www.chinadaily.com.cn/china/2007-05/26/content_880766.htm*

29 Geoff Dyer, *"Wen Dismisses Currency Pressure,"* 27 December 2009, Financial Times website. *http://www.ft.com/intl/cms/s/0/3069c326-f2e5-11de-a888-00144feab49a.html#axzz1dcUNN1YX*

30 Jiang Xufeng, *"China Won't Yield to Yuan Appreciation Pressure,"* 27 December 2009, Xinhua English News website. *http://news.xinhuanet.com/english/2009-12/27/content_12711333.htm*

31 People's Bank of China Statement, *"U.S. Senate's Voting to Consider Currency Exchange Rate Oversight Reform Act of 2011 on October 3,"* 4 October 2011, People's Bank of China website. *http://www.pbc.gov.cn/publish/english/955/2011/20111004174509537934640/20111004174509537934640_.html*

aimed at allowing the Chinese to appreciate the RMB at their own pace without facing punitive action from the U.S.

Lee Taylor Buckley is an alumnus of the Sam Nunn School of International Affairs, Georgia Institute of Technology, Atlanta, Georgia.

Understanding China's Trade Surplus: Going Beyond Currency Manipulation

Sam Trachtman
Vol. 10, No. 2
2011

Introduction

One of the most controversial macroeconomic issues of this decade is the question of how China has run such massive trade surpluses and has accumulated so much in foreign reserves over the past 20 years. Generally, developing countries tend to run current account deficits and capital account surpluses, meaning that on net they import both goods and capital investment, which they repay in later stages of development. The benefit is that they can use developed countries' wealth to fuel domestic investment and growth (Buera and Shin, 2010). China began to follow this strategy at the start of reform and opening in the 1980s. Beginning in 1992, however, domestic demand fell, the economy shifted toward exports, and China began running trade surpluses (Huang and Tao, 2010). While it is natural for some countries to temporarily run current account surpluses and some to run deficits, the magnitude and longevity of China's surpluses are noteworthy, especially for a developing country.

The current account is the broadest measure of a nation's economic relationships with the rest of the world. It puts the value of goods and services in the plus column and subtracts imports and returns on investments abroad. A negative current account balance means a country is importing more than it is exporting. Capital must come into the country to "pay for" the imbalance. Think of it this way: If a household spends $10,000 more than it earns, it must borrow the difference - for example, from a credit card company. The household has a current account deficit and a capital account surplus of $10,000. A country is no different.

If it runs a current account deficit, it must compensate with a capital account surplus. In China's case, the reverse is true. China exports much more than it imports and saves at a high rate rather than buying imports, thereby running large current account surpluses and capital account deficits. The extra money that China earns from abroad gets reinvested, among other places, in U.S. Treasuries.

What explains the unusual trade surpluses China has experienced? A number of factors have been identified as possible causes. Most prominently, the Chinese government's intervention in exchange markets to maintain the RMB-dollar peg has been repeatedly cited as a key factor, since an undervalued RMB would be a type of subsidy on Chinese exports. As when any country pegs its exchange rate, the government maintains the peg by buying or selling foreign reserves to counter market changes in the demand and supply of the domestic currency. Given the demand for the RMB for trade and investment purposes, the Chinese government has been buying foreign exchange, mainly in the form of dollars, and selling RMB to counteract the rising demand for the RMB that would, in a free market system, drive up the value of the RMB (Krugman, 2010). This factor often generates headlines, such as when U.S. Secretary of Treasury Timothy Geithner publicly accuses the Chinese government of currency manipulation as he did in 2010, and when Congress introduces trade sanctions on China in response to currency value assumptions.

The question of whether the RMB is indeed undervalued, as well as whether the undervaluation has a significant impact, is debatable. Cheung, Chinn, and Fujii (2009) use cross-country purchasing power parity samples to evaluate whether the RMB was undervalued in 2006 as well as in 2008. They find the RMB to be five times more undervalued in 2006, yet neither of the tests was statistically significant. The econometric methods used in these tests were also found to lack robustness (Dunaway, Leigh, Li 2006). Moreover, it has been argued that a revaluation of the RMB would not significantly affect current accounts due a likely decrease in imports from Southeast Asian countries that would accompany an increase in exports from the West. The reasoning is that less demand for finished goods from China would cause China to import fewer intermediate goods and raw materials (Garcia-Herrero and Koivu, 2007). Finally, economic theory suggests that to keep its currency persistently undervalued, China would have to cope with devastating inflationary pressures. While inflation has been high, it seems the level of inflation does not reflect the degree to which some argue the RMB is undervalued. In addition, increasing pressures for capital to flow out of China is now suggesting that the currency could indeed be overvalued.[1] In sum, the idea that currency manipulation explains the entirety of the imbalance is not convincing.

---

1   For example, see analysis by the Bank of America; *http://www.zerohedge.com/news/bank-america-charts-four-crash-landing-systemic-endgames-china.*

Other Explanations

A second explanation, the savings-investment gap, suggests that Chinese people have a tendency to save more than they invest, which by definition creates current account surpluses. It could be that the Chinese government's lack of proper social services causes people to save a larger portion of their incomes (Zhou, 2009), or that the underdevelopment of the financial sector causes Chinese to invest a high proportion of their savings abroad, as Corden's "parking" theory argues (2009). While a current account surplus implies savings exceeding investment, it is still a source of debate as to how and why this gap exists.

A third set of explanations for China's large trade surplus beginning in the 1990s focuses on industry and investment relocation. As manufacturing centers moved from Southeast Asia to China through the 1990s and 2000s, especially in final goods production, trade surpluses shifted from Southeast Asia to China (Huang and Tao, 2010). This theory is simple but empirically speaking is not sufficient to independently explain the magnitude of China's current account surpluses over the 2000s. A similar theory proposes that Chinese government domestic policies emphasized growth without first creating a financial system capable of soaking up the excess savings produced by rising levels of national income. One of the most important goals of the central government is maintaining high levels of employment, which causes policymakers to focus on growth (Fan, 2008). The resultant growth yields high levels of savings that, in the absence of a sophisticated financial system with attractive home investment options, end up flooding abroad.

Finally, the demographics theory contends that the high number of Chinese of working age during the 1990s and 2000s resulted in high growth and high savings. The sheer size of the labor force produced excess output, making exports more viable and leading to high levels of national savings, two forces that jointly put upward pressure on current accounts. (Zhu, 2007)

These theories can be divided into those that impact exports and imports and those that impact savings and investment. Currency manipulation and industry relocation quite clearly affect a nation's net exports, while growth policies and demographics theoretically influence both net export and net foreign investment.

Further, these theories are in many ways interrelated, and are certainly not mutually exclusive (Huang). For example, demography, exchange rate policy and pro-growth policy were motivating factors behind the relocation of manufacturing sectors from Southeast Asia to China. Demographics and pro-growth policies also both had an effect on the savings and investment gap. We might even argue that high levels of savings yielded a surplus of RMB, prompting the government to intervene in currency markets through the purchase of dollars. Any attempt to differentiate these effects would likely be in vain.

New Factor Market Distortion Theories

The newest theories of note attempting to explain the source of China's current account surplus revolve around factor market distortions. The issue is explored in Song, Storesletten and Zilibotti's "Growing Like China" (2011), published in the American Economic Review, and Huang and Tao's "Factor Market Distortion and Current Account Surplus in China" (2010), published in Asian Economic Papers. The papers both identify uneven reform policies as the source of imbalances in the Chinese economy. While Song, Storesletten and Zilibotti's model attributes imbalances to the transition from an economy dominated by State Owned Enterprises (SOEs) to an economy powered by private enterprises, Huang and Tao's model considers imbalances in the liberalization of product and factor markets as a type of producer subsidy, which leads to high savings and therefore to high net exports.

The factor market is the market for factors of production. The principal factors of production in any economy are labor, capital and natural resources, but economists have more recently added human capital, intellectual capital and entrepreneurship to this group. Price distortions in factor markets can hugely impact an economy, because factor prices are a significant component in a firm's decision about how much to produce. Huang and Tao (2010), economists at Peking University, argue that asymmetry between China's liberalization of factor markets (the market for inputs) and product markets (the market for goods) cause domestic distortions that directly lead to a current account surplus. Similarly, Song, Storesletten and Zilibotti (2011) construct a model of asymmetries in China's reform and opening in which they show that because China's reform has been characterized by a transition from large SOEs to domestic private enterprises (DPEs), this has contributed to the current account surplus. Because DPEs are less dependent on external financing (financing from outside the firm), the authors argue that this transition reduced investment demand in China, producing current account surpluses.

Song, Storesletten, and Zilibotti's Transition Model

Song et al. begin by considering the question of how China was able to maintain high growth and high return to capital while also sustaining current account surplus and amassing foreign reserves. Neoclassical open economy models would predict high returns to capital to attract foreign investment, causing current account deficits-not surpluses. The authors postulate that China's bucking of the trend could be related to the nature of China's reform. Their model shows that as a reforming economy (for example, China over the past two decades) reallocates resources from inefficient SOEs with access to financial markets to private enterprises with limited access to funding, domestic savings will increase faster than investment, causing a trade surplus.[2]

The authors construct a two-sector model of the Chinese economy, dividing Chinese firms into inefficient SOEs with access to finance and highly efficient private enterprises with limited financial access. Throughout the post-1992 reform period, China's financial sector was still largely controlled by the government. As a result, loans were offered at will to SOEs with necessary connections, but not to private enterprises. According to the authors, SOEs grew inefficient, depending on their liquidity advantage to stay in the market, while private firms were forced to operate very efficiently to overcome financial constraints.

A key assumption for the model is that DPEs will choose to delegate rather than centralize, and young entrepreneurs benefiting from this delegation of responsibility are assumed to choose to invest in the business. Financing for DPEs thus comes from two sources: whatever funding they can extract from the government-controlled financial sector and the savings of entrepreneurs. DPEs will slowly replace SOEs in the economy as entrepreneurs amass higher savings, reducing the importance of the previous competitive advantage held by the SOEs in access to credit. In order for entrepreneurs to be able to save, we must also assume that excess profits are going to managers and owners, rather than to workers. This would lead to growing income inequality, a phenomenon that was indeed observed during the post-1992 reform period (Song et al, p.204).

During transition, as entrepreneurial savings grew, DPEs began replacing SOEs in many industries. The growing prominence of DPEs dependent on self-financing resulted in a reduced demand for domestic borrowing or investment. Recall that SOEs were absorbing the majority of liquidity. Meanwhile, economic growth fueled by DPEs was increasing gross national savings. People were earning more, while fewer people were benefiting from government social programs that reduced the need to save. While SOEs remained a significant part of the economy, their role continually decreased over the reform period. The result, the authors argue, was a high level of savings coupled with low investment demand. Banks were forced to invest extra funds abroad, leading to high current accounts and growing foreign reserves. One of the safest investments for banks was U.S. Treasury bonds, partially explaining how China owns such a large portion of U.S. sovereign debt. Song et al. consider their model to be a superior explanation to currency manipulation for China's high growth and increasing foreign surplus, theoretically exonerating China of currency manipulation.

While the model is convincing in that trends it predicts match up nicely with true developments in the Chinese economy, there are several issues the authors fail

---

2   *Recall that when savings exceed investment, capital will flow out of a country, causing positive net foreign investment and a capital account deficit. Net foreign investment equals net exports, so the country will necessarily then run a trade surplus.*

to resolve. First, the model fails to address the issue of foreign direct investment (FDI). In the model, SOEs are given a low interest rate while DPEs are unable to obtain financing. If the returns to capital during reform were higher than the domestic real interest rate, as the authors' model implies, FDI would theoretically flood in, correcting for the imbalances that theoretically created current account surplus. During the post-1992 reform period FDI into China did indeed increase rapidly (Garcia and Koivu, 2007, 17). The authors might respond that while FDI did increase, it was still regulated, maintaining imbalance in the credit market.

Second, at late stages of reform, when DPEs had already surpassed SOEs as the Chinese economy's main source of growth, why would the government continue to maintain barriers limiting the amount of savings that could be invested domestically, where the returns are highest? In other words, it does not really make sense for the government to have continued to restrict financing for DPEs well into the reform period without some ulterior motive. One explanation, though, is that the motivation to continue to impose financial constraints came from maintaining the RMB's peg, an issue considered in forthcoming sections.

Asymmetric Market Liberalization

A second paper looking at the factor market side, Huang and Tao's 2010 "Factor Market Distortions and Current Account Surplus in China," takes a different angle. Rather than considering frictions in the financial market as the source of imbalance, the authors focus on asymmetries in the reform of factor markets. In simple terms, their argument poses that asymmetric liberalization caused artificially low factor prices (for capital and labor) as compared to product markets, which made export of goods more economically viable. The artificially low factor prices acted as an implicit tax on workers and capital owners, reducing consumption and increasing savings. Huang and Tao argue that these two effects in concert increased the savings-investment gap and the export-import gap, boosting China's current account surplus.

Huang and Tao begin with the observation that in the modern Chinese economy 95% of goods prices are determined by free markets, while the markets for factors of production such as labor, capital, land and energy are still highly regulated. The regulation, they argue, lowers factor prices below market levels, acting as an implicit subsidy for producers. In effect, producers pay a reduced price for factors, but are able to sell their products at near-market prices. This dynamic would lead to imbalances that are reflected in persistent current account surpluses.

In the labor market, China's Hukou (household registration) system results in migrant workers often being paid below their marginal product, or the true value they contribute to production. Migrant workers from the countryside are not eligible for benefits or labor protections. As a result, abundant cheap labor is readily available. In the capital market, as emphasized in the previous paper, the government-controlled financial system continues to offer low interest loans to SOEs, while regulating foreign investment and loans to DPEs. The authors argue that this results in an artificially low real interest rate. Regarding natural resource inputs, the authors show that the government often offers land to Party members with connections rather than through a true market system. In addition, the central government controls prices of other important inputs, such as energy, and keeps that price relatively low for major producers. (Huang and Tao, 2010, p.23)[3]

Artificially low factor prices not only act as a subsidy for producers, but also as a tax on laborers and owners of capital. This tax reduces consumption, which by nature increases savings as a fraction of income. The authors argue that this contributes to the savings-investment gap.

In summary, Huang and Tao argue that government regulation in factor markets subsidizes industry production while taxing labor and capital. The subsidy effect increases net exports at a given exchange rate, while the tax increases net foreign investment at a given real interest rate through its effect on savings, jointly causing current account surplus. The strength of the paper is that it points to one element that is clearly observed in the Chinese economy that affects both the export-import gap and savings-investment gap that contribute to current account surplus.

On the other hand, it is unclear whether the government's interference in the financial market, the market in which the authors estimate the largest distortion, subsidizes or taxes production. The authors argue that government regulation of financial markets artificially lowers the price of capital, subsidizing production. However, Song et al. demonstrate that the regulation also decreases the liquidity available for DPEs, the major source of growth in the Chinese economy. If this were the case, it would seem that government interference on aggregate may have an ambiguous effect on producers, helping enterprises that have connections, but hurting most private firms without access to funding. Given that financial markets are estimated to contain the largest distortions, this ambiguity is troublesome for the authors' results.

Furthermore, if the Hukou system were reformed and labor mobility improved, while certain industries may be forced to pay higher wages, it may on aggregate benefit economic production. The reasoning is that greater labor mobility would allow workers to seek out industries in which they are most productive. In sum, whether the imperfections illuminated by the authors concretely act to help producers, or whether their effects are ambiguous, is crucial. If the effects

---

3   *Huang, in a separate 2010 paper attempts to estimate the scale of the market distortions. He finds distortion to total RMB 2.1 trillion in 2008, with capital, or financial, market distortions making up the lion's share (Huang, 2010).*

are ambiguous, the model does little to explain China's current account surplus.

Conclusion

The current account balance reflects import-export and savings-investment dynamics. The two models analyzed above jointly have explanatory power regarding both of these dynamics. Song et al. demonstrate how financial frictions during the reform period caused lower investment demand and higher savings. Huang and Tao consider imperfections in Chinese factor markets as producer subsidies, causing excess production that affects the import-export dynamic. In this sense, these models can be seen as complements.

As far as how these models relate to the earlier theories explaining trade surpluses, they are not mutually exclusive. However, the relationship between currency manipulation theories and factor market distortion theories does prompt a chicken-egg question.

It could be argued that by pegging the RMB to the dollar at an artificially low rate, the Chinese government has forced itself to introduce subsequent imperfections. The financial market is a good example. Both papers discuss how interest rates are artificially low in China. The theory posed in Song et al. depends on the assumption that the Chinese financial market exhibits certain frictions. As open-economy models tell us, pegging one's currency necessitates loss of control over domestic real interest rates. It could be that financial market imperfections that form the basis for these theories arise out of the government's maintenance of an artificially low currency peg. Perhaps the reason that the government limited DPEs' access to credit was to reduce demand for the RMB and maintain the peg. This reasoning would indicate that revaluing the currency would correct the imbalances in the economy that produce persistent trade surpluses. The authors, though, claim that their theory shows currency revaluation is not a magic bullet.

On the other hand, it could be that market imperfections of the sort illuminated in Song et al. and Huang and Tao caused currency intervention policies. Perhaps the government ended up having to purchase U.S. Treasury bonds because of the excess savings predicted in the "factor market distortion" models. If this is the case, the government should worry less about revaluing and more about fixing internal market imperfections. Deciding which phenomenon causes the other is extremely difficult. In reality, the currency intervention and factor market distortion are likely closely intertwined.

The observations made in both Song et al. and Huang and Tao's papers are helpful in understanding the source of China's high current account surpluses throughout the 2000s. While it is difficult to know the true magnitude of the effect of the theoretical imbalances the papers describe, they provide a conceptual framework for understanding Chinese current account surpluses outside of the tired currency manipulation narrative. There are indeed deeper issues at play. In this vein, China should focus both on managed exchange rate revaluation and reducing domestic financial frictions and factor market distortions to correct imbalances in the future. Moreover, the U.S. government should understand that the root of imbalances likely digs deeper than simple currency controls.

References

Huang, Yiping, and Kunyu Tao. "Factor Market Distortion and Current Account Surplus in China." *Asian Economic Papers.* 9.3 (2010)

Song, Zheng Storesletten, Kjetil and Zilibotti, Fabrizio. "Growing Like China." *American Economic Review.* (2011) 196-233.

Krugman, Paul. "Chinese New Year." *New York Times* 31 Dec 2010.

Corden, Max. "China's Exchange Rate Policy, Its Current Account Surplus and Global Imbalances." *Royal Economic Society.* (2009) 103-199.

Dunaway, Steven, Leigh, Lamin, and Li Xiangming. "How Robust are Estimates of Equilibrium Real Exchange Rates: The Case of China." *International Monetary Fund.* (2006)

Garcia-Herrero, Alicia and Koivu, Tuuli. "Can the Chinese Trade Surplus be Reduced Through Exchange Rate Policy." *Bank of Finland Discussion Papers.* (2007)

Buera, Francesco and Shin, Yongseok. "Productivity Growth and Capital Flows: The Dynamics of Reforms." *National Bureau of Economic Research.* (2010)

Huang, Yiping and Wang, Bijun. "Cost Distortions and Structural Imbalances in China." *China and the World Economy.* (2010)

Cheung, Yin-Wong, Chinn, Menzie David and Fujii, Eiji. "China's Current Account and Exchange Rate." *National Bureau of Economic Research.* (2009)

Zhou, Xiaochuan. "Some Observations and Analyses on Saving Ratio." *People's Bank of China.* (2009)

Fan, Gang. "Debating China's Exchange Rate Policy, Commentary." *Peterson Institute for International Economics.* (2008)

Zhu, Qing. "Analysis on Chinese Special International Income and Expenditure Structure." *World Economy Study.* (2007)

Allen, Franklin, Jun, Qian, and Mei, Qian. "China's Financial System: Past, Present, and Future." "The Transition that Worked: Origins, Mechanism, and Consequences of China's Long Boom." (2005)

Yongding, Yu. "Global Imbalances and China." *Australian Economic Review.* Vol. 40, p. 2-23.

"China's Trade Surplus to Shrink this Year, Deficits Likely for Some Months." English.xinhua.com. Xinhua, 03/07/2011. Web. 26 Apr 2011. .

"China posts a surprise trade deficit as exports slow." *BBC News* . BBC, 12/03/2011. Web. 26 Apr 2011. .

Frankel, Jeffrey, Wei, Shang-jin. "Assessing China's Exchange Rate Regime." *National Bureau of Economic Research.* (2007)

Sam Trachtman majored in economics at Pomona College and served as an intern in China in 2010 and at the U.S. Treasury in 2011.

Developing Western China: Xi'an's Maturing Economy and the Role of Producer Services

Susan M. Walcott and Chen Ying
Vol.9, No.1
2010

Xi'an, famed for its Terracotta Warriors of ancient times and as a strategic interior location in Maoist China, is rising again, as a provider of producer services.

Historic Roots

Xi'an's importance as the major city in central western China extends from its history as the imperial capital of China, anchoring the eastern terminus of the Silk Road, to its current status as the capital of Shaanxi Province and a major destination for both tourism and high technology development. The famous Terracotta Warriors – Great Wall architect and Emperor Qin Shi Huangdi's lifelike funerary soldiers and horses – as well as the nearby Banpo excavations of some of China's earliest archaeological finds, attest to the site's strategic location at a fertile bend of the Yellow River. Beyond its agricultural riches, as the ancient imperial capital Xi'an functioned as a wealthy Silk Road entrepot for trade with lands from India to Rome. The impressive mosque constructed to honor Moslem mariner Admiral Cheng Ho in his hometown still attracts worshippers, another lingering sign of Xi'an's role as a doorway from Han China to the Western lands.

Following the Communist victory in 1949, elements in the PRC's leadership became concerned over the perceived vulnerability of mainland China's east coast cities to an invasion. A series of interior secondary cities were chosen as a "Third Line" for the relocation of technical research universities and strategic industries. These later formed the basis for Xi'an's rise to new regional prominence around the turn of the 21st century.

The three main components of modern Xi'an's producer services sector are financial services (banking, insurance and securities), information consulting (advertising, lawand accounting), and computer services (software, data processing and database services). In the decade from 1997-2006, employment in Xi'an's financial services firms increased from 30,000 to 43,000 employees; information consulting employment almost doubled from a 60,000 base; and computer consulting doubled from 16,000 to 32,000. Clearly, Xi'an's service-based economy, also referred to as the tertiary sector, was experiencing lift-off.

New Urban Patterns

As in the east coast economic powerhouse cities of Shanghai and Guangzhou, the location of Xi'an's service sector is largely the result of State intervention. To accommodate a new concentration of highly educated, skilled and relatively affluent residents, Xi'an launched major construction projects for office parks, research centers, middle-class and upscale housing, and accompanying amenity landscapes. New city quarters took shape predominantly on the south side of the city and in dedicated space within the old walled city, the traditional central business district. Also catering to the tourist trade of increasingly affluent Chinese as well as foreigners, a shopping mall close to new hotels sprang up (complete with a Starbucks offering local market flavors such as red bean coffee). Urban planners installed a mock-up of new Xi'an in the lobby of its largest high-tech industrial park headquarters, featuring trendy greenbelts and park spaces such as seen in Shanghai's new modern urban showcase of Pudong and the Zhangjiang high-tech Park.

Key universities with promise for research breakthroughs in commercial areas were chosen as investment targets. These institutions were then provided with extra funds, enlarged, and in many cases moved to new campuses. The new locations were often developed in tandem with nearby high-tech parks to house hoped-for spillover businesses based on breakthrough products. Xi'an Jiaotong University's high-tech park pioneered this concept in western China, which Chengdu's Sichuan University used in turn as its model. Examples of such development include special facilities for students returning from at least one year of education abroad, with ideas for promising practical research projects, and business incubators for fledgling entrepreneurs.

Economic Bases of Development

A traditional model of economic development consists of five stages: primary level extractive activities such as agriculture, fishing, or mining; secondary-level manufacturing activities; a tertiary level of services provision; a quaternary level of occupations involving knowledge creation; and quinary-level command and control functions. A maturing, increasingly developed economy shifts its economic function concentration up the ladder of these stages, though progress is not perfectly linear. China's predominance at the secondary stage does not mean that it is less advanced than India, whose economic modernization focuses on tertiary-sector service occupations.

However, while China is widely hailed as the 'factory of the world' for its manufacturing prowess, Chinese economic planners have expressed concerns since the 1990s that the country's most advanced urban centers lacked a significant tertiary sector. Central government funding began to target what were seen as the roots of a new growth-inducing base for more innovative, higher skilled and higher paying jobs.

Xi'an High Tech Park Headquarters

China has sought to fund economic modernization based on promoting innovative industries through a number of schemes such as the Spark Plan, the 863 Plan, the Torch Plan, and several other technology-targeted programs. China's service sector is based more on domestic innovations and firms than India's, which is linked more with global foreign companies. For China this promises more return on investment through less leakage outside the immediate area. Following proclamation of the "Develop the West" policy, Xi'an became a major target for accelerated attention along with Chengdu and Chongqing. From 1997 to 2006, the industrial output value of Xi'an's service industry increased at an annual average rate of 13.74%, compared to traditional service industries of 0.74%, and represented a growth from US$8.113 billion to US$25.85 billion.

Producer Services

Producer Services form a prominent sector within the services category. Increasing in importance since the 1960s, producer services emerged as an important function of Xi'an's economy starting inthe 1980s. Firms in this sector serve manufacturing, business and government needs rather than sell directly to individual consumers. Their location is not tied to the traditional downtown central district, but needs to be close to their business customers and in the vicinity of high-speed Internet lines due to their information-intensive nature. Firms engaged in producer services are often housed in office towers, since the expense of telecommunications infrastructure makes this a congenially concentrated footprint. The growth of producer services accompanied the external substitution of service functions formerly performed in-house. Reasons for externalization include cost as well as expertise; the increasingly complex nature of business requires complex services, from financial to computer consultants. This condition has been found to be particularly positive for promoting localized growth within highly populated metropolitan regions anchored by advanced cities.

The location pattern of Xi'an's producer services subsectors varied by proximity to their target market. Financial services cater largely to decision makers engaged in the processing of information for the traditional FIRE (finance, insurance, real estate) companies that occupy a concentrated nucleus in the central business district. Information consultancy services concentrate close to their clients in the southside university and research park region, as well as in the central business district. Due to the particular need for fast communication, computer services are the most agglomerated along the southern research periphery of knowledge-intensive industries.

To illustrate its development stature, Xi'an also acquired a new pedestrian mall, though less bustling than Beijing's Wangfujing or Shanghai's Nanjing Road complex " but still a statement of retail strength for a west China inland city in a largely poor province. As in Chengdu, another major western city with a new pedestrian mall area, nightlife can be more vibrant than during the day when many workers are occupied.

Construction of new university sites, predominantly on the south side of Xi'an where relatively inexpensive land was available, allowed signs to emerge of new cultural and social patterns. The newly relocated Shaanxi University campus, which retains its older site closer to the central city, sports a towering new statue in front of the massive library: China's rehabilitated sage Confucius. According to several students and faculty questioned concerning the prominence of this decidedly post-Cultural Revolution figure, Confucius' distinction lies with his promotion of education.

Implications for Xi'an's Future

Government policy – pouring funds into key western China locations in order to stimulate the development of future wealth in the services sector--seems to have been successful in Xi'an. This metropolis managed to retain important parts of its visible history in the form of pavilion towers and a uniquely intact wall around its old urban center. Outside the surrounding moat, new Xi'an features glass office towers largely occupied by the new services sector. Among the most important of these are the featured producer services, mirroring and sustaining the strength of its economically pioneering and relatively advanced client firms. The orderly and rational nature of the agglomerated producer service and client companies along Xi'an's southern boundary indicates the power of state-level urban planners to complement economic construction with physical infrastructure, creating a reinvigorated oasis of affluence in the dry lands of west China.

Susan Walcott, Ph.D. is professor of geography, specializing in economic geography and Asian Studies, at the University of North Carolina, Greensboro. Chen Ying, Ph.D. is professor of geography at Shaanxi Normal University in Xi'an, specializing in urban geography.

The Neoliberal Sunshine in Northwestern China: A Case Study of Government Sponsored Job Training Programs, Migration, and Poverty Alleviation in Gansu and Ningxia Provinces

KuoRay Mao, Kay Kei Ho Pih and Shuming Bao

Vol. 9, No. 2
2010

Introduction

Since the advent of economic reform in China, the Chinese government has channeled most of its resources to the development of its coastal provinces. Northwestern China has lagged behind in infrastructure and economic development. The poverty associated with geographical limitations and decades of resource extraction policies in these provinces has created significant economic stagnation in the region. In the 2000 Chinese Census, two thirds of the officially defined poor households were located in western China (The World Bank 2001). Starting in 1999, the western development policies have injected much needed capital into the northwestern provinces and have promoted structural changes in the rural economy in the region. The shift of rural labor out of crop production has been much faster and greater in its magnitude compared with other regions in China (Du et al 2005). Based on the 2009 Western China Migration and Labor Resources Survey (CMLRS), we explore several factors related to rural-urban migration and social stratification in Northwestern China. We find that the migrant labor regime within the neoliberal framework does little to alleviate poverty because the regime has failed to increase capital accumulation in rural villages in Northwestern China. To develop its northwestern region, we suggest that the Chinese government further lessen its control over the hukuo, or household registry system, to allow greater migration between the village and township levels.

The Neoliberal Turn

Chinese reform since 1978 has coincided with the emergence of neoliberal ideology in the world. Since the collapse of the Fordist-Keynesian regime in the 1970s, a new model of production, flexible accumulation, has dominated the global market. As flexible accumulation expanded, high levels of structural unemployment and rapid destruction and reconstruction of skills became prevalent conditions in the labor market. The reliance on part-time, outsourced labor further weakened the strength of labor unions and nation states in relation to the flow of capital (Harvey 1991:150, 170). The ever present drive to shorten the return time on profit in the expansion of a capitalist economy demands the constant compression of time and space in production and consumption patterns. With rapid development in information technology, the acceptable turn-around time for capital accumulation decreased. The subsequent changes in relations among capital, labor, and state-induced manifestations of a schizophrenic condition, where the present triumphed over history, eliminated the sense of continuity and coherence in social lives around the world.

Neoliberal development tends to focus on short-term financial gain instead of long-term stable growth. As capital becomes a circulatory process of commoditization, consumption, and accumulation, the resulting phenomenon of "accumulation by dispossession" leads to an enhancement of the position of elites at the expense of the working class (Dicken 2007; 343). Globally, most countries that adopt neoliberalism have experienced increases in social inequality and the concentration of economic and political power to the upper classes (Harvey 2007:48-50). Neoliberal capitalism invariably creates a debacle in which debt-financed growth has to simultaneously depend on eliminating employment opportunities for efficiency while increasing consumption from the bottom. The end result has been a global shortage of jobs. According to Dicken (2007), in the next decade, the global economy needs to create at least 400 million new jobs in addition to the volatile, flexible (read part-time) positions that already exist (450). In developing countries, massive underemployment is appearing due to the growth of labor that far exceed the limitation of the "Green Revolution" in the agricultural sector (511). In China alone, it is estimated that 15 million jobs need to be created every year as rural surplus labor accounts for close to 62% of the total labor force (Ash 2009).

Migrant Labor Regime

True to the neoliberal ideology, China's astronomical growth in GDP is based on the exploitation of the "migrant worker regime," the most flexible employment arrangement possible. Rural migrant workers fill the lower tier of the split labor market. China's rural surplus laborers fit into the neoliberal framework which "requires a large easily exploited and relatively powerless labor force and is vulnerable to super exploitation" (Harvey 2007: 127,144). Migrant workers tend to work in assembly line positions and in construction while workers with urban registration status enjoy welfare coverage from the state and the upward mobility to join the burgeoning middle class. The enduring division between urban hukuo holders and temporary migrants, in terms of different life expectations, has demonstrated that rural migrants remain excluded from full participation in urban society in both living conditions and social welfare provisions (He et al 2008). Research has repeatedly demonstrated that migrant workers still suffer from a multitude of discrimination and blocked upward mobility in cities across China (Ash 2009, Du et al 2005, and Fan 2008). Compared with the rural population, people with urban registration enjoy significant advantages in resource allocation and life chances. The inequality of opportunity embedded in the hukou system has invariably contributed to severe social stratification between the countryside and the urban areas, which has propelled massive rural to urban migration, especially after Deng's tour of the southern Special Economic Zones. According to Harvey (2007), the dire condition of the rural sector and the instability associated with rapid urbanization is one of the most serious problems facing the Chinese government (Harvey 2007: 127). It was estimated that from 1995 to 2004, between 5 million and 6 million peasants joined the army of 150 million migrant workers in the city each year (Harvey 2007: 140). And a recent report by the Chinese Academy of Sciences points out that in order to alleviate poverty in rural areas the government needs to relocate "500 million rural dwellers to cities and to facilitate the movement of 600 million city dwellers into the suburbs" (Dicken 2007:227).

Rural migration from hinterland regions to cities in coastal provinces has long alleviated rural poverty in China. The differences in development between the coastal and hinterland region are primarily due to the concentration of Township and Village Enterprises (hereafter TVEs). More than 80% of gross rural income in China comes from non-agricultural activities, and close to 60% derives from rural industry alone (Ash 2009). However, these TVEs are mostly concentrated in coastal provinces. In the northwestern region, the industrial manufacturing sector contributes only slightly over 5% of gross rural income (Du et al 2005). This lack of industrial development has resulted in massive rural underemployment in the Chinese Northwest. In 2004, it was estimated that rural surplus labor levels in Gansu and Ningxia stood at 61.6% and 58% respectively (Ash 2009). The geographical concentration of the underemployed in the countryside creates "contextual inequality" in which the life chances of individual peasants are constrained by the lack of economic opportunities regardless of personal traits (Wilson 2006). In 2004, the average personal income in the northwestern region was less than 48% of that in coastal provinces (Ash 2009). This pattern of social stratification is even more profound when rural areas are included in the comparison. In 2004, net rural income in eastern China was 91% higher than that of western China (Du et al 2005).

Migration, Capital, and Poverty Alleviation

The connections among local migration policy, migrants' remittances, expansion of social networks, and the development of local economies affect patterns of migration within migrant sending communities (Du et al 2005). In Northwestern China, pressures of population on limited arable land and the increasing arid climate push the local ecological system to critical thresholds. Perplexingly, numerous surveys since 2000 indicate that the northwestern region has the lowest percentage of rural to urban migration compared with other provinces in China, even though western development policies have drastically improved infrastructure. Existing literature on migration and stratification often involves close examination of capital available to people living in different social contexts. According to Bourdieu (1986), capital can be viewed as resources accessible to individuals to facilitate social action (241). Different forms of capital are interconnected and are translatable into each other. Possession of one form of capital facilitates and enhances the acquisition of other types of capital. Social stratification among different sectors therefore cannot be alleviated simply by increasing the human capital of the bottom while opportunity hoarding and disparity in political power remain. As the state bureaucrats and rogue capitalists consolidate political representation, the increasing rural-urban divide and disparate regional development have become pressing issues in regards to the stability of the Chinese neoliberal system in Northwestern China.

To alleviate the severe poverty and to ameliorate regional disparity, in 2004, the Ministry of Agriculture initiated the "Sunshine Project" to provide job training programs to potential rural migrants in the Northwestern region. In some poor counties designated as models for migration of surplus labor, the county governments go beyond providing information for employment opportunities or job training. They are responsible for directing potential migrants to specific industries and establishing national "brand awareness" for their migrant workers. Government-sponsored job training can be conceptualized as a form of social capital that generates human capital in each migrant worker. This poverty alleviation measure is a good example of the top-down mobilization often employed by developmental states in the neoliberal system. Therefore, it is interesting to examine how intervention by the state into the labor market affects patterns of migration and social stratification 10 years after the initialization of the western development policies.

Data

We used data from the 2009 Western China Migration and Labor Resources Survey (CMLRS) to examine the effects the western development policies exerted on migration patterns and rural economies in Northwestern China. The CMLRS covered three western provinces: Sichuan, Gansu, and the Ningxia Hui Autonomous Region. It was conducted from April to July 2009 and sampled 741 households and more than 3,400 individuals in these provinces. For the purpose of this study, we conducted bi-variate correlation analyses on data from Gansu and Ningxia. We hypothesized that:

1. Those who received more education and government-sponsored job training were more likely to migrate. We wanted to explore whether the infusion of resources via top-down mobilization of the neoliberal state actually increased human capital and provided chances of employment for each migrant worker. In other words, can interventionist measures lessen the rural-urban divide, which has long inhibited the formation of a unified labor market in China?

2. Migrants with higher education or those receiving government training were more likely to have higher personal income and send more remittances to their households. We wanted to study whether investment in human capital through from top-down mobilization actually benefited individual workers and migrants originated from rural villages in Northwestern China.

3. Individuals from ethnic minority counties were more likely to migrate and to rely on personal networks to obtain information on employment. Given the unique ethnic situation in Northwest China, we wanted to find out whether the migrant labor regime was embedded differently in the ethnic context from that of the Han community and how this difference might influence patterns of migration.

Discussion

Results from the bi-variate analyses are somewhat consistent with our hypotheses. As expected in Gansu and Ningxia, individuals between the ages of 14 and 60 are more likely to be associated with migration. Notably, government-sponsored job training is significantly associated with migration. In fact, government-sponsored job training appears to be the most important variable in the preliminary analyses. From the cumulative causation theoretical perspective, government-sponsored training can be treated as a form of social capital which facilitates migration. The training, network, and organization provided by the county government, significantly increased the human and social capital of individual migrants. The state's policy consequently represents a major source of capital influencing migration patterns in China. According to Zai et al (2008), the effect of migrant social capital on migration is not necessarily uniform across settings and may be shaped by public policies in the sending or receiving community contexts. The clear division in our data in migration patterns between counties with and without officially sponsored migration policies clearly supports the literature.

Table I. Kendall's Tau b Coefficients

	Age	Gender	Education	Migration	Government Sponsored Job Training
Age	1.00				
Gender	.029	1.00			
Education	.424**	-.171**	1.00		
Migration	-.321**	.167**	-.203**	1.00	
Government Sponsored Job Training	-.308**	.17588	-.198	.792**	1.00
** Coefficient is significant at .01 levels (2 tailed). (n = 2,351)					

A negative association between government-sponsored training and income and remittance is slightly perplexing. A negative association between education and migration is also unexpected. It appears that government-sponsored job training and education were significant only when it comes to the decision to migrate. The association between government-sponsored job training and migration is the strongest in the binary analyses. As soon as individuals migrate, education and government-sponsored job training seem to have weak or no relation to income or remittance. The data therefore support hypothesis one but reject hypothesis two. The great majority of people in rural areas are not able to finish high school (Wu and Trieman 2007). They often become migrant workers after junior high or attend vocational schools with questionable learning environments (Fan 2008:97). Wu and Trieman (2007) state that contrary to past research indicating high upward mobility in Chinese society, there is actually a strong downward mobility in the rural sector. The limited upward mobility in rural areas is only available to those who scored high in college entrance exams and have the means to attend universities to switch their hukou to urban status.

Table II. Kendall's Tau b Coefficients of Migrants

	Education	Government Sponsored Job Training	Income	Remittance
Education	1.00			
Government Sponsored Job Training	.037	1.00		
Income	1.43**	-.304**	1.00	
Remittance	.041	-182**	.578**	1.00
** Coefficient is significant at .01 levels (2 tailed). (n = 2,351)				

Due to the underdevelopment in the rural economy in the region, limited career options are available to individuals with rural hukou. Government-sponsored job training becomes an attractive alternative to individuals who do not have the opportunity to obtain a high school education and beyond (Knight and Tueh 2009). However, government-sponsored job training and government-organized migration typically are focused in construction, manufacturing, and low-end service sector jobs (Snyder and Chern 2009). These jobs provide little upward mobility in the emerging "hourglass" economy and generate little return on investment in human capital such as education and job training (Wilson 1997:224). Fan and Stark (2008) further state that without regulation, a government's effort to increase educational expenditure and thereby the number of skilled workers may result in decreased wage rates in both rural and urban areas. Our findings reflect the literature on the low return of investments in migrants' human capital (Snyder and Chern 2009).

Meanwhile, the literature suggests that individuals who remain in their place of origin generally come from backgrounds with household incomes considerably higher or lower than the poverty line (Du et al 2005). Those who remain and have the access to work in non-agricultural jobs such as in local TVEs and the retail sector tend to have higher net incomes than migrant workers (Snyder and Chern 2009). Our findings support this pattern as well. In addition to the effects of the hukou system, the negative association between education and migration can be preliminarily attributed to the economic and employment patterns on the local level. The different outcomes in income between individuals may be related to whether individuals have the means to attend high school or are constrained to government-sponsored training. Even when migrants received government-sponsored job training, the aforementioned correlations suggest that they are more likely to be associated with lower incomes and remittances. Interestingly, the negative association between training and income is stronger among those who stayed (b=-.916**, r=-.925**) than those who migrated (b=-.304**, r=-.406). In other words, those who received government-sponsored training and failed to migrate may have the lowest income compared to migrant workers and people who attended high school and stayed. Thus, the data indicate that there is a strong difference in upward mobility between those who have the opportunity to attend high school and those who are directed to the vocation training track.

Our findings on gender corroborate with the latest literature on migration and stratification in China. According to Fan (2008), young males and females in rural areas tend to migrate at a similar rate even thought they tend to go into different employment sectors (47). Since the loosening of the hukou policy, there is also an emerging trend of married couples migrating to the same destination within a short period of time (He et al 2008). Contrary to the literature, our analyses find no significant association between distance to a major city and migration. County governments' involvement in organizing migrant labor may be a factor as many of the organized seasonal migrant workers in Ningxia and Gansu are sent to petroleum production sites and cotton fields in Xinjiang and in Qinghai (Interview Notes). We are surprised to find that there is no significant association between migration and ethnicity and ethnic networks and employment opportunities. We speculate that lineage and local networks may be stronger social capital than ethnicity in social organization in the Chinese rural society.

Conclusion

The data show how government-sponsored job training is highly associated with the decision to migrate. Interestingly, the analyses show education is negatively associated with migration, which can be attributed to the skewing effect of the hukou system and patterns of job allocation in the local political economy. We find that once individuals migrate, education and government-sponsored job training seem to have weak or no relation with income or remittance. This result suggests that migration propelled by government-sponsored job training can be a short-term solution for surplus labor in rural areas of the northwestern region; however, it produces little progress in the long term development of the local economy. Therefore, we believe that the migrant labor regime within the neoliberal framework does little to alleviate poverty in Northwestern China. Job creation and investment in TVEs in the rural area may be a better approach to poverty reduction in the region. However, given the fragile condition of the region's ecology, industrial development will likely lead to further desertification and pollution and therefore limit the human and social capital available to local residents.

Based on our findings, we believe that development driven by unconstrained GDP growth as typified by the migrant labor regime is detrimental to the long term stability of the region. The unique ecology and ethnic diversity of Northwest

China cannot sustain the external and social cost often associated with neoliberal policies in developing countries. In addition, the post-socialist institutional transformation in the region is severely behind the coastal provinces. The regional economy is dominated by state-owned enterprises. Private enterprises are weak and congregate in the service sector. This uneven distribution of resources and market opportunities inhibit innovation and tend to encourage rent-seeking behaviors from high level managers and bureaucrats who, as invested actors, are likely to continue the track of unsustainable development.

One alternative is to have the state provide tutelage and support for a circular economy by encouraging government R&D investment and providing tax incentives to the renewable sector in Northwestern China. Instead of the continued reliance on resource extraction and on energy/labor intensive industries as streams of revenue, regional governments should gradually shift their development strategy to green industries at the township level by utilizing land resources and surplus labor from rural areas. To increase capital accumulation in rural areas, the state should further lessen hukou registration by encouraging urbanization as the township level. Currently, to transfer a hukou from rural to urban status, one has to give up the right to lease farm land in one's original village. The circulatory nature of migration is often interrupted and consequently remittances dwindle as migrants opt to stay and spend their income in cities where they are employed. The exodus of working age people creates a vicious cycle of poverty as people who stay behind cannot gain income from migrants' consumption and the rural areas lose the opportunity to accumulate capital. The government can consider allowing recently urbanized peasants to keep their land-lease rights, thus encouraging migrants to work and stay in adjacent townships and stimulating capital flow toward surrounding villages. Lastly, given that sustainable development has become a major theme with the 12th Five Year Plan, the central government in Beijing needs to reduce differences in policy implementation for the central, regional, and local levels to avoid the agency issue in governance, which has long exacerbated social stratification and polluted local environments in China.

References

1.   Ash Robert 2009 "Employment and Migration: A Chinese Rural Perspective" in Resurgent China: Issues for the Future edited by Nazrul Islam. Palgrave Macmillan: London
2.   Bourdieu, Pierre. 1986 "The forms of capital" In J. Richardson" Handbook of Theory and Research for the Sociology of Education Greenwood Publishing: New York, 241-258
3.   Dicken Peter 2007 Global Shift: Mapping the Changing Contours of the World Economy 5th edition Guilford Press New York
4.   Du, Yang, Albert Park, Sangui Wang 2005 "Migration and Rural Poverty in China" Journal of Comparative Economics 33 688-709
5.   Fan Cindy C.2008 China on the Move: Migration, the State, and the Household. Rutledge: London.
6.   Harvey, David 1991 The Condition of Postmodernity: an Enquiry into the Origins of Cul-

tural Change Wiley-Blackwell; Reprint edition

7. _____*2007 A Brief History of Neoliberalism Oxford University Press, USA*

8. He, Shenjinglkjd; Yuting Liu; Fulong Wu and Christ Webster 2008 *"Poverty Incidence and Concentration in Different Social Groups in Urban China, a Case Study of Nanjing" Cities Vol. 25 121-132*

9. Snyder, Steve and Wen S Chern 2009 *"The Impact of Remittance Income on Rural Households in China" China Agricultural Economic Review Vol. 1 No 1 38-57*

10. The World Bank 2001 *China: Overcoming Rural Poverty. The World Bank: Washington DC.*

11. Wilson, William Julius 1991 *When Work Disappears: The World of the New Urban Poor Vintage: New York. New York*

12. Wu, Xiaogang and Donald J Treiman 2007 *"Inequality and Equality under Chinese Socialism: The Hukou System and Intergenerational Occupational Mobility" AJS Volume 113 No. 2 415-45 September*

Kuo Ray Mao is a graduate student at the University of Kansas; Kay Kei Ho Pih, Ph.D., teaches sociology at California State University-Northridge, and Shuming Bao, Ph.D. is the Director of the China Data Center at the University of Michigan.

City and Rural Commercial Banks in China: The New Battlefield in Chinese Banking?

Vijaya Subrahmanyam

Vol.10, No.1
2011

Introduction

China's vast rural areas and lesser known cities have become a focus of attention both for China's banking industry and foreign banks. A major signal of this trend came in 2010, when AgBank of China, one of the country's major banks, made an IPO that became known as the manna from heaven for the nation's western, rural regions. The bank is now aiming at narrowing the gap with the affluent coastal areas.[1, 2] Foreign banks, such as Canada's Bank of Nova Scotia and Spain's two largest banks, BBVA and Banco Santander, are increasingly investing in smaller Chinese banks in the hope of profiting from rapid growth in the financial sector. Banco Santander, in fact, agreed to take a 19.9 percent stake in a joint venture with China Construction Bank Corp. to provide banking services outside China's major cities, according to The Wall Street Journal. Much of the interest by Chinese and foreign banks is focused on China's City Commercial Banks (CCBs) and Rural Commercial Banks (RCBs), which largely serve small and medium-sized businesses sprouting up across China.

There are other indications that CCBs and RCBs could become the focus of a new wave of expansion in the Chinese financial sector. In December 2010, Chongqing Rural Commercial Bank, one of China's largest lenders to farmers

---

1   *A note of thanks to Maya Nyayapati from Monta Vista High School, Cupertino, CA who assisted me in researching the literature for this paper.*

2   *Oliver, Chris, "Some market players wary of AgBank's massive IPO," Market Watch, Wall Street Journal, July 7th, 2010.*

and small businesses, raised US$1.48 billion in an IPO in Hong Kong in what is expected to be the first in a wave of listings by smaller rural-focused Chinese banks.[3] In addition, four Chinese RCBs in east China's Jiangsu Province have won approval from the country's banking regulator for their IPO plans. China's Banking Regulatory Commission (CBRC) said it encouraged and supported qualified rural financial institutions to pursue listings.[4]

A focus on rural areas and smaller cities could help ease the yawning and growing gap between China's largest cities and the countryside. Despite China's rapid urbanization, particularly in coastal provinces, the majority of China's total population still lives in rural areas.[5] China's rural-urban wealth gap has been an issue of concern, with the average annual income for a rural worker around RMB 5,150 ($750) while those in the cities earned RMB 17,180 ($2,510) on average in 2009.[6] A recent study showed that the current banking system meets only about 60 percent of rural household financial needs, and about half of rural agricultural needs.[7]

This research focuses on assessing CCBs and RCBs as vehicles for easing gaps in China's economic development and as a sector of interest by foreign investors. The essay will include an explanation of the services they provide to growing and yet underserved small and medium-sized firms found in smaller cities and rural regions and an analysis of how and why foreign banks are looking to invest in these lesser known Chinese banks.[8] The first task is a brief history of CCBs and RCBs.

Background

In 1995 the first of the CCBs came into existence with the key aim of boosting local economic development and small and medium enterprises (SMEs). China's CCBs are joint-stock commercial banks established by local governments, enter-

3   *Wall Street Journal, "Chongqing Rural Raises $1.48 Billion in IPO", Dec 9, 2010. http://on-line.wsj.com/article/SB10001424052748703766704576009033364363062.html?KEYWO RDS=Chongqing+Rural+Commercial+Bank*

4   *Pei, Yan, "Rural commercial banks step up listing plans," January 21, 2011, China.org.cn, http://www.china.org.cn/business/2011-01/21/content_21794212.htm*

5   *CIA World Fact Book*

6   *People's Daily Online, "Government to address urban-rural income gap", September 11, 2010, http://english.peopledaily.com.cn/90001/90776/90882/7137089.html*

7   *Kwok, Vivian Wai-yin, "Let 1,000 Rural Banks Bloom in China," Forbes.com, 2009. http://www.forbes.com/2009/07/30/china-rural-bank-markets-financial-reform.html*

8   *This study is focused only on the formal sector although it may be useful to note that there is perhaps a large informal sector that would not be included in the official data bases which are used in this research. A recent Financial Times article (Sender, Henry, "Chinese finance: A shadowy presence," Financial Times, March 31 2011) reported about the shadowy presence of an informal lending sector in China noting that in response to the heavy hand of the regulators, a host of grey-market institutions and arrangements has sprung up to circumvent formal restrictions in China's heavily controlled financial markets.*

prises and residents. These banks sprouted from shareholding reform and former urban credit cooperatives. They are allowed to open branches only within their home cities. Few of the CCBs have any private investment capital and have largely been used to finance local government projects. They are thus influenced by local governments, which are perhaps more bureaucratic and less developed than the central government. CBRC reports indicate that these banks are largely present to grant loans to SMEs that operate within city boundaries.

Several RCBs have been created since 2001 in order to improve financial services in the countryside. The four RCBs of Zhangjiagang, Wujiang, Changshu and Jiangyin have received approval for an IPO and, along with Chongqing RCB's IPO in Hong Kong, they have placed RCBs in the forefront of China's banking industry. Since the CBRC revised regulations covering rural banking in 2006, allowing foreign banks to operate alone or with partners, HSBC, Standard Chartered and City have all established their presence in China's interior.[9]

In a move to further close urban-rural income gap, the Banking Commission and the Chinese government are planning to increase the number of RCBs more than tenfold to 1,027 by the end of 2011. This development will be particularly focused on central and western China, where most people are farmers with little access to financial and loan services.[10]

The CBRC actively encourages foreign banks to engage in business with small and medium-scale enterprises, but most foreign banks believe these endeavors are relatively risky, and their financial information is not transparent. In addition, foreign banks lack the networks required to reach them. Thus an alternate route has been to invest in or create alliances with CCBs. Under similar encouragement from the CBRC, foreign banks are also increasingly involved with rural banking via RCBs. This helps them establish links across the nation in a more tangible fashion and meet the needs for banking services in the rural areas.

Research increasingly notes that it is beneficial for foreign lenders to team up with a CCB or RCB.[11] CCBs and RCBs benefit both directly from capital investments as well as from knowledge transfer gained from experienced management and financial innovations in products and services obtained from foreign partners. CCBs and RCBs also benefit indirectly by being able to offer superior products and services that make them more competitive in the domestic market. In turn, these alliances with Chinese banks could potentially result in further endeavors

---

9   Kwok, Vivian Wai-yin, *Let 1,000 Rural Banks Bloom in China, 2009, July,* Forbes, http://www.forbes.com/2009/07/30/china-rural-bank-markets-financial-reform.html

10   Qing, Zhang Xiao, "THE CHINA COLUMN: rural banking - a new battlefield, 15 July 2010, http://news.efinancialcareers.cn/newsandviews_item/newsItemId-27087

11   Hope, Nicholas C., Laurenceson, James and Qin, Fengming, 2008. "The Impact of Direct Investment by Foreign Banks on China's Banking Industry," Working paper No. 362, Stanford Center for International Development, April.

for foreign banks. They not only are an easier route for foreign banks, but they also help the banks grow organically with local incorporation. Recently, Australia and New Zealand Banking Group Ltd. (ANZ), one of Australia's top lenders, announced plans to invest in China via expansion of its branch network and seeking local incorporation.[12] At present the bank owns a 19.9 percent stake in Shanghai RCB and a 20 percent stake in Bank of Tianjin, a CCB. Other banks in Australia also similarly hold stakes in CCBs. This is expected to lead to a rush of second-tier regional banks from the West investing in China with the intent of expanding into less urbanized areas.

City Commercial Banks

Recent research has been mixed on the performance of CCBs. A 2007 KPMG study noted that China's banking sector assets grew at a compound annual growth rate of about 13 percent since FY 2000 reaching a massive $3.8 trillion; CCBs account for five percent of that total.[13, 14] The study also shows that their performance has been less than stellar with poor capital adequacy, high non-performing loans (NPLs) and limited market penetration. Consequently, these banks have had regulatory mandates to reduce their NPLs to 15 percent by 2005 and maintain an eight percent capital adequacy ratio (CBRC, 2006 Annual report). In their defense, more recently, Giovanni Ferri (2009) finds that while CCBs have low market share, they boast of high growth and better performance than the State Owned Commercial banks (SOCBs). In addition, he points out that while their performance was a mixed bag, they had a 13.2 percent growth in assets in 2005, and their ROEs and ROAs were still higher than those seen in SOCBs. Ferri's paper, although recent, was based only on a small sample of CCBs for which data was available in Bankscope.[15]

By 2005, there were 113 CCBs. That number rose to 140 by FY 2009. By the end of 2005, the average capital adequacy ratio of China's CCBs was 5.14 percent, and the number of CCBs with the capital adequacy ratio up to eight percent rose to 36 from 18 in early 2005. CCB NPLs totaled RMB 84.2 billion in 2005, decreasing by RMB 21.7 billion in 2004, and loan quality improved; only

---

12   *Wei, Michael and Alan Wheatley, Foreign banks again hear the call of China, Reuters, Feb 2 2010; http://www.reuters.com/article/2010/02/02/us-dealtalk-china-banking-idUS-TRE61116320100202*

13   *Opportunity knocks, KPMG, 2007*

14   *Asian Wall Street Journal, "City Lenders offer foothold for international investors in fast growing market," Feb 2005. CBRC, 2005; KPMG Report, "China's City Commercial Banks: Opportunity Knocks? 2007.*

15   *BANKSCOPE is a complete financial analysis tool, combining information on 11,000 world banks with a financial analysis software program. The information includes detailed spreadsheet data (balance sheet and income statements), ownership information (shareholders and subsidiaries), Reuters news articles, ratings and rating reports. The data is updated 18 times a year.*

7.7 percent were non-performing in 2005, four percentage points less than the previous year and down from 30 percent five years previously. (CBRC Reports, 2006).[16]

From 2006 to 2009, according to official Chinese statistics, CCB assets almost doubled.[17] During this time both the average growth in assets as well as the share of CCB assets in proportion to all banking institutions rose each year (see Table 1 on page 70). This perhaps reflects the growth of Chinese SMEs creating an increased need for CCBs.

Fourteen of these 140 banks had assets that exceeded RMB 100 billion, more than 50 percent (70 banks) had assets of RMB 10 billion-100 billion and more than 50 banks held less than RMB 10 billion (CBRC report, 2009-10). The NPLs in China's banks had been in decline by 2005 and continued a downward trend from 2006 to 2009. The average outstanding balance on loans of RMB 75.8 billion had gone down to almost half of that, or RMB 46.2 billion, by FY 2009. Also, in contrast to the aforementioned KPMG (2007) study, the proportion of NPLs as a share of total loans declined in all commercial banks, and in CCBs, NPLs went from 6.29 percent of total loans in 2006 to only 1.76 percent in 2009, steadily declining each year (see Table 2 on page 77).

What has caused CCBs' improved performance in the latter years, and is that performance sustainable? CCBs' major advantage lies in that they are local, with capital and ownership derived from the communities they serve. They are expected to become prominent players in the future of China's banking landscape since private enterprises in China – mostly SMEs – produce some 52 percent of GDP but account for only 27 percent of outstanding loans.[18] Ferri (2009) finds that the performance of CCBs is significantly and positively related to the level of economic prosperity in the provinces where they are located. They have recently thus attracted foreign banks that are seeking strategic investment opportunities in China. The improved performance (decline in NPLs) may be a result of increased competition perhaps resulting in more efficient performance.

---

16 *Official statistics from the CBRC cover only the formal banking sector, and are subject to China's definitions of specific categories which sometimes differ from international standards. Official statistics, however, tend to be generated by required periodic reporting and government surveys, so often have reliable coverage.*

17 *Chow (2006), not referencing CBRC in particular, points out that Chinese official statistics are by and large reliable because of the assigned responsibility of the officials preparing them, of their being used in government decision making that is open to public scrutiny, and in many published articles in referred journals. He cautions the reader of typical errors of omission or statistical discrepancies as in any data. Gregory Chow, 2006, "Are Chinese Official Statistics Reliable?," CESifo Economic Studies, Oxford University Press, vol. 52(2), pages 396-414, June.*

18 *Putting China's Capital to Work: The Value of Financial System Reform, McKinsey Report, May 2006. http://www.mckinsey.com/mgi/reports/pdfs/china_capital/MGI_chinacapital_exec-sum.pdf*

Table 1: City Commercial Banks' Quarter-end Balance, RMB 100 million, %

FY		Total Assets	YoY Growth Rate	Share*	Total Liabilities	YoY Growth Rate	Share*
2006	Q1	20,886.70	25.3	5.30	20,054.10	24.7	5.40
	Q2	22,986.00	27.8	5.60	22,073.60	27.2	5.70
	Q3	24,207.20	28.5	5.70	23,194.40	27.9	5.80
	Q4	25,937.90	27.4	5.90	24,722.60	26.5	5.90
Average		23,504.45	27.25	5.63	22,511.18	26.58	5.70
2007	Q1	26,806.40	28.3	5.8	25,491.20	27.1	5.8
	Q2	29,176.50	26.9	6.0	27,800.00	25.9	6.0
	Q3	30,905.80	27.7	6.1	29,188.80	25.8	6.1
	Q4	33,404.80	28.8	6.4	31,521.40	27.5	6.4
Average		30,073.38	27.93	6.08	28,500.35	26.58	6.08
2008	Q1	33,953.70	26.7	6.1	31,915.10	25.2	6.1
	Q2	35,921.60	23.1	6.2	33,801.80	21.6	6.2
	Q3	38,868.80	25.8	6.5	36,542.00	25.2	6.5
	Q4	41,319.70	23.7	6.6	38,650.90	22.6	6.6
Average		37,515.95	24.83	6.35	35,227.45	23.65	6.35
2009	Q1	44,888.60	32.2	6.5	42,116.50	32.0	6.5
	Q2	49,547.00	37.9	6.7	46,609.30	37.9	6.7
	Q3	52,103.70	34.1	6.9	48,886.90	33.8	6.9
	Q4	56,800.10	37.5	7.2	53,213.00	37.7	7.2
Average		50,834.85	35.43	6.83	47,706.43	35.35	1.

Source: China Banking Regulatory Commission Report
* Note: "Share" means the proportion of the city commercial banks to all the banking institutions.

In a recent Pricewaterhouse Coopers (PWC) survey, foreign banks note that despite an increasing threat from domestic banks, China's market appears extremely strategic with the expectation of aggressive development. As they expand into China's large market base of lenders and focus on the SMEs, will they be able to sustain their growth?

Rural Commercial Banks

RCBs regard SMEs as their key clients to provide them with business operations aimed at serving the agriculture sector and other rural industries. Histori-

Table 2: Commercial Banks' Non-Performing Loans (NPL) as of end-year, 2006-09

Commercial Banks	Share in Total Loans				Average NPL Share in Total Loans	Average Outstanding Balance
	Q1	Q2	Q3	Q4		
2006						
Major	8.26	7.80	7.64	7.51	7.80	11819.2
City	7.59	6.72	6.07	4.78	6.29	758.1
Rural	6.96	6.64	6.58	5.90	6.52	155.85
2007						
Major	7.02	6.91	6.63	6.72	7.02	11614.2
City	4.52	3.95	3.67	3.04	4.10	659.6
Rural	5.32	4.80	4.21	3.97	5.06	150.6
2008						
Major	6.30	6.00	6.01	2.45	5.19	11782.2
City	2.90	2.72	2.54	2.33	2.62	508.8
Rural	3.68	3.26	4.44	3.94	3.83	129.5
2009						
Major	2.02	1.74	1.64	1.59	1.75	4427.9
City	2.17	1.85	1.70	1.30	1.76	461.95
Rural	3.59	3.20	2.97	2.76	3.13	214.55
Source: China Banking Regulatory Commission Report.						

cally, bank lending to rural areas has not performed on par with lending to urban areas. In order to encourage banking to rural areas, the CBRC and central government have considered new incentives such as tax cuts, lowered capital requirement for rural banks, and subsidy programs that include infrastructure development, some of which have already been initiated.[19, 20] This effort has not gone to waste. Table 2 shows a dramatic jump in average outstanding loans for RCBs in 2009 and a definite reduction in NPLs over time showing movement in the right direction. The recent Agbank IPO and Zhangjiagang RCB IPO approval of December 2007 may improve the outlook for RCBs.[21]

In December 2010 Chongqing RCB, the largest bank in the municipality, was the first Chinese mainland-based rural bank to list on the Hong Kong Stock

---

19 http://www.chinadaily.com.cn/business/2011-04/07/content_12287075.htm
20 Gale, Fred, "Financial Reforms Push Capital to the Countryside," *The Chinese Economy, 42* (5), Sep-Oct 2009, 58-78.
21 AgBank IPO Faces its Next Challenge, Wall Street Journal, July 28, 2010.

Exchange.[22] Upon its debut it did not perform to par, and its shares later fizzled in trading, reflecting skepticism among Chinese investors. However, it marked an important point in Chinese banking since it is expected to be the beginning of an era of similar listings by RCBs and CCBs in Shanghai and Hong Kong as these banks look to the markets to bolster their balance sheets and raise capital for expansion.[23] It is also a test to gauge foreign-investor interest in the growth of China's hinterlands. RCBs may be seen as a means to provide capital to rural areas, and foreign banks may find RCBs an easier way to penetrate rural markets, which still require extensive networks. Evidence of such is noted with banks such as ANZ Bank, which not only opened a rural branch near Chongqing last year but also has a 20 percent stake in the Shanghai RCB as well as in Banco Santander SA's joint venture with China Construction Bank Corp. in rural banking. The future may lie there if a viable operating model can be developed to control risk and manage non-performing loans by perhaps requiring adequate capital.

Unfinished Agendas

In China, alongside a huge untapped market for financial services, many challenges still face both the CCBs and the RCBs. Banks operating in the inner provinces and in the rural banking market are faced with a lack of experience, lack of talent and the high costs of building infrastructure and networks. With the newer economic policies, foreign banks are increasingly attracted to CCBs and RCBs as a strategic option to penetrate the Chinese banking market thus diversifying their portfolios while simultaneously limiting their investment and hence risk.[24] So far, foreign banks in China have displayed lower NPLs as a share of total loans than local commercial banks. Non-performing loans have gone from 0.87 percent of total loans in 2006 to 0.74 percent in 2009. Thus CCBs and RCBs are increasingly looking to foreign banks as a boon rather than a bane since this may be their opportunity to expand by obtaining more access to capital while simultaneously learning about new products and adapting new strategies without having to re-invent the wheel. In December 2007, HSBC became the first foreign bank to set up a rural bank in China and now has seven rural branches; the largest network among the overseas banks. Richard Yorke, HSBC's former China CEO, recently commented: "The rural banking sector is under banked, so we are seeing strong demand for the right product and for the right services. There is strong untapped

---

22   *IPO Tests Taste for Rural Growth, Wall Street Journal*, Nov 30, 2010; "*Chongqing Rural Commercial Bank gains 3.8 percent at HK debut,*" *China Daily*, Dec 16, 2010.

23   "*Chongqing Rural raises $1.35 billion in HK IPO: sources*" by Kevin Soh and Denny Thomas, Reuters, HK, Dec 9, 2010; http://www.reuters.com/article/2010/12/09/us-chongqing-pricing-idUSTRE6B81F720101209

24   http://www.pwc.com/tw/en/challenges/invest-in-mainland-china/invest-in-mainland-china-20100608.jhtml

demand in that market.";[25] Katherine Tsang, China CEO of rival Standard Chartered, has also said that her bank's first rural branch in Inner Mongolia has been running better than expected. "Rural banking is a long-term commitment and we are not in a rush to make quick money. We will set up more rural banks, if the first one proves to be a role model."[26]

Alongside typical transactional issues, Chinese banking is rampant with issues such as lack of transparency, government interference, non-productive assets, NPLs and lack of technical know-how among others. As one ponders the future of Chinese banking, many of these issues need to be addressed both for the CCBs and RCBs that intend to expand, and foreign banks that plan to expand into China via mergers with these institutions. Strong support from the Chinese government and more incentive policies to support RCBs and CCBs are needed and may help with their long term sustainability and the future of Chinese banking.

References

Ferri, Giovanni, "Are New Tigers supplanting Old Mammoths in China's banking system? Evidence from a sample of city commercial banks," *Journal of Banking and Finance*, 33, 2009, 131-140.

Gale, Fred, "Financial Reforms Push Capital to the Countryside," *The Chinese Economy*, 42 (5), Sep-Oct 2009, 58-78.

Brough, Paul, "China's City commercial banks: Opportunity Knocks?," KPMG, 2007.

Vijaya Subrahmanyam, Ph.D. is professor of finance at the Stetson School of Business & Economics, Mercer University, Atlanta, GA.

---

25 Qing, Zhang Xiao, "THE CHINA COLUMN: rural banking - a new battlefield, 15 July 2010, http://news.efinancialcareers.cn/newsandviews_item/newsItemId-27087

26 Ibid.

New Words and Novel Usages: An Analysis of Marketing Vocabulary Used by Chinese Online Shopping Websites

Hong Li and Shanshan Wang
Vol.11, No.1
2012

Introduction

In recent years online shopping has grown rapidly in China. According to Sina, online commerce has become an important sector in China's economy, accounting for 3% of total retail volume in 2010 (Sina).

Among the many factors that contributed to this success: innovative language used by online shopping websites, particularly new vocabulary and novel usage of words. This paper presents an analytical study – from marketing and linguistic perspectives – of language that has played a pivotal role in attracting customers and promoting products.

Research on the language of advertising in English that examines vocabulary used in television and commercial publishing, has effectively related the use of words with functional factors of advertising such as capturing attention, listenability, readability, memorability and selling power. Geis (1982) made an attempt to describe how language is used in American advertising, particularly in television advertising. He concluded that advertisers in general tend to prefer vague language to language with explicit empirical consequences, and they opt for subjective claims rather than objective claims. Mencher (1990) looked into the aspect of vocabulary in advertising and identified key personal and persuasive words.

There have also been many articles scrutinizing Chinese advertising language from various perspectives, such as studies on advertising discourse (Guowen Huang, 2001) and pragmatics of advertising language (Junyuan Wang, 2005). Wang (2005) studied the marketing effects of novel usage of fixed expressions, such as four-character proverbs, folk sayings and idioms. He pointed out fixed expressions are used creatively in commercials by either changing their linguistic form or meaning. He argued that this type of novel usage of common expressions is effective in advertising because it grabs people's attention with its freshness and familiarity and leaves a deep impression.

Since the popularity of online shopping is relatively recent in China, research on advertising language used by online stores is lacking. This paper aims to fill this gap by focusing linguistically on new vocabulary and novel uses of words on online shopping websites. The authors have collected data from China's most popular business-to-customer and customer-to-customer websites from January 2008 to March 2012. It is hoped that this study can shed light on the language features of online marketing.

Linguistic Features of New Words and Collocations

Internet advertising shares few qualities with its equivalents in newspapers, magazines and on television. It is an electronic, global and, most importantly, interactive format. Both sellers and consumers control the effectiveness of Internet advertising. Since "behavioral response and branding are two major objectives of Internet advertising," (Li & Leckenby 2004: 25) it must meet customers' needs for information, entertainment and value, by using a variety of elements including innovative use of language, multiple forms of media and interactivity. In China, more than "90% of netizens are below the age of 35. In other words, Chinese netizens can be roughly categorized as young people." (Gao 2008: 362) The interactive nature of Internet advertising and its target population determine that the language used must be engaging and innovative.

In China, new online shopping websites open on a daily basis. Competition among them is becoming fiercer. To stay competitive and generate more traffic, these websites must aggressively advertise their products and special deals, particularly before important holidays such as National Day, Christmas and Chinese New Year. New words and expressions and novel usages of existing words are used to catch potential customers' attention and provoke action.

New Words

Vocabulary is probably the most versatile component of language. New words are consistently created to meet the needs of communication. In China, according to Gao (2008: 373), some of the Chinese Internet Lexicon (CIL) usages "have already been used by the general public and beyond the modality of CMC (computer mediated communication)." Among Chinese Internet Lexicon, many of the words originated from online shopping websites.

New Words Originated from Names of Websites

Some words originating from online shopping websites are becoming new words in the Chinese language and are used in daily communication.

Take Táobǎo 淘宝 ("to pan for treasure") as an example. It is the name of the largest online shopping website in Asia with more than 370 million registered users as of the end of 2010 (China Daily). As an indisputable leader in e-commerce, the word táobǎo has become a household expression, referring to a shopping strategy in which one goes through numerous stores online or off-line to find the best deals. Below are two examples:

1) 有市民向记者传授淘宝经验，虽然商家都说不能还价，但大多还是有讲价余地的。

(Citizens tell reporters about their experiences of panning for treasures. Although some businesses say that the prices are non-negotiable, in fact in most cases it is possible to negotiate the price.) (07SShz)

2) 山东商报社区淘宝节将再次来到天桥区。

(The Taobao Community Festival, hosted by Shandong Business Newspaper, will come to Tianqiao District again.) (WTOOW)

The word táobǎotǐ 淘宝体 ("taobao style") is another new word related to the online shopping website. It originated from the writing style of describing products or special deals on its website. Such descriptions usually begin with qīn 亲 ("dear") and then adopt an informal, personalized, intimate tone. The popularity of this style of writing has caused some traditionally formal or official communications to adopt taobao style. The following examples illustrate this fact:

3) 亲们，淘宝社正式招新啦！

(Dear All, the Taobao community is recruiting!) (Nanjing College of Information Technology)

4) 南京理工大学录取通知使用淘宝体。

(Acceptance notices to incoming freshmen from Nanjing University of Sciences and Technology adopt the Taobao style.) (ifeng.com)

New Words Originated from New Marketing Strategies

In November 2010 wánpāi wǎng 玩拍网 (www.wanpai.com) was launched. As its name suggests – wán 玩 ("to play") and pāi 拍 ("to auction") – this website is a unique platform combining social networking with online auctioning. Different from traditional auction websites on which shopping for deals is the only goal, users of this website can make and connect with friends, and play games while participating in online auctions. In addition, this website uses a variety of innovative auctioning methods, offering either zero-dollar or extremely low starting bids and allowing customers to decide how much they are willing to pay. This website quickly grew to be China's leading auction website. As a result, more competitive bidding websites have established. The new word jìngpāi 竞拍 ("competitive bidding") has also become widely used.

1) 百元竞拍一触即发，长城平板，笔记本抱回家.

(Competitive bidding at 100 RMB quickly became viral. People brought home flat screen desk tops and laptop computers.) (yesky.com)

2)   当晚的拍卖现场颇为热闹，许多图书出版公司的出版人赶来竞拍。

(The auction scene this evening was quite lively. Many publishers came to participate in the bidding.) (Chinanews.com)

The term miǎoshā 秒杀 ("sec kill") denotes another popular sales strategy. According to baidu.com, miǎoshādiàn 秒杀店 ("sec kill store") on www.taobao.com is the website's most popular feature (Baidu).

The word miǎoshā 秒杀 was officially included in the Ministry of Education's 2007 new word list (Baidu). At the time, however, the word was used in the context of computer games, referring to a strategy of attacking opponents. It wasn't until around 2010 that the word became a popular term for online shopping. It refers to a promotion in which potential buyers go to a website at the same time and hit the "order" or "buy" button in quick succession. Deep discounts are awarded first come, first served and the process takes mere seconds, hence the "sec(ond) kill" reference.

Many other related words have been invented highlighting its popularity.

3) miǎopiào 秒票 ("to buy tickets using the sec kill strategy")

4) miǎoshāqì 秒杀器 ("sec kill device")

New Collocations

In terms of linguistic codes, some of the new words used on online shopping websites are mixtures of either Chinese characters and English letters or words or mixtures of purely Chinese characters. This type of lexicon is not restricted to the context of online shopping. It is in fact one important feature of Chinese Internet Lexicon (CIL). (Gao, 2008)

Hold zhù hold 住 ("to maintain, to hold on to")

Hold 住 was originally a Cantonese word. It became a popular online word in Mandarin Chinese in the summer of 2011 after a participant on a Taiwanese reality TV show used it repeatedly in her comedy performance (Sina). As an online shopping term, it can be used by both sellers and buyers. When used by sellers, it is either for the purpose of influencing and tempting buyers into taking action or for highlighting the advantages of the promotion. Below are some examples.

良无限, hold 住全场的性比价

(We have an unlimited number of excellent products! These goods provide more bang for your buck than you will find anywhere else.) (Taobao.com)

Hold 住夏季体重，中药减肥正当时

(Take charge of your weight this summer! Now is the time to lose weight with the help of Traditional Chinese medicine!) (Rayli)

JM们 ("sisters")

"JM" represents the Pinyin initials for jiějie 姐姐 ("older sister") and mèimei 妹妹 ("younger sister"). Combining the English letters JM with the character for plural form men 们, the term JM 们 is commonly used in online posts by and for females. The term adds a layer of intimacy and creates a sense of community. One example is listed below:

护肤精华露那些事，JM 们快来看！

(Sisters, come and take a look at these skin care products!) (Onlylady)

In addition to shopping websites, consumers – particularly young female shoppers – often use the word to post product information for other female friends, as shown in the example below:

最新消息，国内唯一的OTC减肥药—奥利司他胶囊，品牌名好像叫做"雅塑"，已经在在国内上市了! 这下JM们有福啦,我们再也不用费尽周折从国外代购奥利司他了！

(This is the latest news. The only OTC weight loss drug, Orlistat Capsules, are now available in China. This is indeed a blessing for sisters! We won't have to go through the trouble of buying from abroad.) (ifeng.com)

In addition to these English-Chinese hybrids, online media has also created some purely Chinese collocations. Below are a few examples.

jìnbào zhíjiàng 劲爆直降 (powerful and explosive price cut)

gěilì jùxiàn 给力巨献 (awesome and gigantic promotion)

gěilì fàngsòng 给力放送 (awesome giveaway)

Innovative and Unusual Usages of Existing Words
Idiomatic Expressions

Online shopping websites often use Chinese idiomatic expressions in unexpected, creative and sometimes proactive ways. Because idioms are highly compact and rich in meaning, using them in advertising achieves the purpose of conveying more information in limited words. Additionally, using them in creative ways adds another layer of meaning, thus attracting people's attention.

Chīhēwánrlè 吃喝玩乐 ("eat, drink and be merry") is an idiom describing indulgence in eating, drinking and having fun. During the holiday shopping season of 2011, however, online shopping websites used this expression to promote their holiday sales. Using yìyuán miǎoshā 一元秒杀 ("one Yuan sec kill") as a marketing strategy, the promotion called chīhēwánrlè 吃喝玩乐 included deep discounts and coupons for beauty salons, restaurants, theaters, gyms and travel. In this holiday shopping season, chīhēwánrlè 吃喝玩乐, an idiom with negative connotations, was transformed by being given an atmosphere of merriment and celebration. To enhance the call for action, the website Taobao created a sales area titled ChīhēwánrlèGO 吃喝玩乐GO. The word "go" referred to travel packages, as in going somewhere, in addition to images of energy, vigor and liveliness.

Yìwǎngdǎjìn 一网打尽 ("to catch all in one net") is another idiom used in shopping websites. In this proverb, wǎng 网originally refers to a fishing net. However, when used by online shopping websites, it gains another layer of meaning, referring to wǎngluò网络, the Internet. The proverb thus shows that this website has everything one needs. It is used either to highlight the comprehensiveness of information and goods or to lure customers into buying large quantities or varieties of goods. Below are some examples:

1) 南京新闻，本地报纸，广播，电视，新闻一网打尽。

(Get news about Nanjing from local newspapers, TV and radio on one website.) (Longhoo.net)

2) 合肥购物网，打折、服饰、家电、美容信息一网打尽。

(Hefei online shopping website where you can find everything you need, such as discount clothes, household appliances, electronics and beauty products.) (gou-wu.hefei.cc)

Another sales promotion around the 2011 Chinese New Year was xīnnián dàsǎochú 新年大扫除 ("the New Year clean-up"). One of the great traditions of Chinese New Year is to clean house and put things in order as a way to sweep out the old to usher in the new. On shopping websites such as Taobao, this term was used as a banner for cleaning and personal hygiene products right before the Chinese New Year.

Dúyīwú'èr 独一无二 is a proverb meaning "unique." The advertisement changes the second character yī 一 ("one") into yī 衣 ("clothing"). Since the two characters have the same pronunciation, the proverb's sound is unchanged, so it retains its original meaning when spoken. However, as a clothing advertisement, this change highlights the sales items in the proverb, signifying that the products and the sales are unique and hard to come by.

New Meanings of Existing Words

Some words gain new meanings on shopping websites.

Shài 晒 ("to share")

In *A Modern Chinese-English Dictionary*, the verb shài晒is described as "to shine upon" and "to dry in the sun, to bask." Its meaning strictly indicates actions related to the sun. In the Internet era, the semantic scope of this verb is greatly expanded to refer to a wide range of activities online. Basking in the sun, the root meaning of shài晒, implies the absorbance of sunshine and heat, practices considered beneficial and enjoyable. Similarly, when used online, shài晒metaphorically refers to information sharing among Internet users, ranging from shài gōngzī 晒

工资 ("sharing salary"), shài qínggǎn 晒情感 ("sharing feelings"), shài gōngzuò 晒工作 ("sharing work experiences"), shài yù'ér jīng 晒育儿经 ("sharing chid bearing experiences") and shài gòuwù jīng 晒购物经 ("sharing shopping experiences"). The purpose of information sharing online is to focus on the interaction and community-building among Internet users.

Shài 晒 is also frequently used as a verb on online shopping websites. Some websites generate shopping lists, (i.e., gòuwù shàidān 购物晒单) "to promote clearance or sales items" on míngpǐn dǎogòu wǎng 名品导购网 (mplife.com).

Bài 败 ("to buy")

Bài 败 ("to fail") is used in place of the verb mǎi 买 ("to buy"), because it is similar in pronunciation to the English word "buy." Some websites' names use Bài 败, such as bàiwùnǚ xiǎo wěiwěi 败物女小炜炜 (Taobao.com), a flagship store on Taobao's website. Below are some examples:

帅爸甜妈必败夏装情侣装纯棉挂脖连衣裙男背心-相亲相爱

(Lover's outfit! Skirt and shirt for sweet parents! A must-buy for the summer!) (PaiPai)

内地游客香港必败化妆品推荐

(We have recommendations for cosmetics for Mainland tourists to Hong Kong.) (zhuguo.com)

Linguistic and Rhetorical Features
Word Choices

One common feature in word choices is the use of emotive and strong adjectives that can stimulate extreme emotions and desires.

Fēng 疯 ("crazy")

One of the most common words used by online shopping websites is fēngqiǎng 疯抢 ("to snatch crazily"). Examples include táobǎo quánmín fēngqiǎng 淘宝全民疯抢 ("everyone shop madly on Taobao") and tuángòu fēngqiǎng 团购疯抢 ("mad snatching by group-shoppers").

Bào 爆 ("explosive")

Bào 爆 forms the word bàokuǎn 爆款 ("products that are in high demand"). Bào 爆 is also used in jīngbào jià 惊爆价, referring to extremely low prices that are surprising and newsworthy.

Rhetorical Devices
Figures of Speech

The use of figures of speech is a common and universal advertising technique. In a survey of 24,00 ads, 75% used at least one figure of speech (Leigh 1994). On Chinese shopping websites, one common type of figure of speech are those related to war and violence. These figures of speech shock people into paying attention and becoming energized, encouraging them to buy products.

In December 2011, before Christmas and the Chinese New Year, many shopping websites started sales promotions called xǐyíng shuāngjié bèizhàn niánhuò 喜迎双节，备战年货 ("Happily awaiting the double holiday and stocking up on New Year goods"). The word bèizhàn 备战 literally means to prepare for war. In this context, it was used metaphorically to stress the intensive shopping rush to get ready for the holidays. It added a sense of urgency and intensity.

Exaggeration

The use of exaggeration is also a traditional advertising technique. It over-emphasizes properties of products – be it their prices, functions or styles – to the extreme, encouraging consumers to buy them. On online shopping websites, words are often used in literary and exaggerated ways to promote sales. As shown in previous examples, adjectives such as fēng 疯and fēngkuáng 疯狂 are often used in adverbial position to modify verbs, thus exaggerating the emotive aspect of the actions. Jù 巨, meaning "huge," is used to exaggerate the scope and benefits of promotions, as in jùhuì 巨惠, jùxiàn 巨献, and jù huásuàn 巨划算.

Pun

Puns are amusing uses of words or phrases that have two meanings. Called the game of words, puns leave a deep impression on readers by their readability and humor. The nature of puns in advertising is nicely captured by Attridge. "The pun is the product of a context deliberately constructed to enforce an ambiguity, to render impossible the choice between meanings, to leave the reader or hearer endlessly oscillating in semantic space." (Attridge 1988) Keenly aware of the limits of a computer screen display, shopping websites employ puns to maximize the information conveyed to customers.

One unique type of pun is to combine the brand name with the general meaning of the word. It conveys the product information, as well as the meaning of the word. One famous example is the advertisement for Lenovo computer:

人类失去联想，世界将会怎样?

(What the world would be like if man loses Lenovo?) (Baidu)

In this advertisement, liánxiǎng 联想 is the brand name of Lenovo computer. At the same time its general meaning of associating ideas and thoughts is also employed. It makes readers think about the world without Lenovo and the world without man's ability to think in connected ways. In addition to effectively using puns, this advertisement also resembles lines of poetry in the number of characters and rhyme structure. It is thus catchy and easy to remember. Lenovo's ad was so popular it inspired similar ads from other companies, such as the one seen below:

人类失去苹果，世界将会怎样？

(What the world would be like if man loses Apple?) (IT Time)

Discussions and Conclusions

The rapid expansion of online shopping markets has provided vitality for China's e-commerce and the Chinese language. Many of the new words and usages on shopping websites are vivid, dynamic and sometimes witty. They seem to appeal to e-shoppers, mostly people in their teens and early 20s.

In addition to their popularity, the new words quickly adapt to changes in e-commerce and marketing strategies. Lastly the new words also reflect changes in social and cultural spirits in China. One notices that the new expressions serve to build and maintain online communities and help establish net users' identities. New address terms such as JM们 use kinship terms to address site visitors, thus shortening the distance between the online stores and their customers and generating the feeling of a big family.

Since online shopping websites attract millions of users, particularly young people, the impact of the new vocabulary and novel usage of words cannot be underestimated. Some of the expressions already have been used by the general public, even beyond the modality of shopping websites. As demonstrated in this paper, lively and vibrant new words – particularly when used by young people who are regarded as "in the vanguard of most [language] changes" (Wardhaugh 1998: 202) – have the potential to become integral parts of the Chinese language and contribute to linguistic changes.

The generation and development of the new Chinese marketing vocabulary also has had several negative impacts. For example, most words come from the more profitable and influential online shopping websites. Websites that are less profitable and popular tend to copy the popular words used on major websites and as a result create confusion among consumers. The quality of the products often does not match the description, generating dissatisfaction and complaints.

Despite the mixed effects on new words and novel usages on China's online shopping websites, one cannot ignore their popularity and increasing influence on communication, particularly among the younger generation. Due to their potential impact on language change and development, they warrant more linguistic research.

References
1. A Modern Chinese-English Dictionary. Beijing: Foreign Language Teaching and Research Press, 1992
2. China Daily. "Taobao Split into Three Companies," 2011. Web. 22 May 2012. http://www.chinadaily.com.cn/bizchina/2011-06/17/content_12720292.htm
3. Gao, Liwei. "Language Change in Progress: Evidence from Computer-Mediated Communication." Proceedings of the 20th North American Conference on Chinese Linguistics (NACCL-20): 1 (2008): 361-377.Web. 16 May 2012. http://chinalinks.osu.edu/naccl-20/proceedings/19_gao_l.pdf
4. Geis, Michael. The Language of Television Advertising. New York: Academic Press, 1982.

Print.

5. Leigh, James H. 1994. "The Use of Figures of Speech in Print Ad Headlines." Journal of Advertising 23. 2 (1994): 17-34. Print.
6. Li, Hairong, and John D. Leckenby. "Internet Advertising Formats and Effectiveness." An invited Chapter for Thorson & Schumann (2004): n. pag. Web. 16 May 2012. http:// brosephstalin.files.wordpress.com/2010/06/ad_format_print.pdf
7. Madura, Jeff. 2006. Introduction to Business. 4th ed. Mason: Thompson Higher Education, 2006. Print.
8. Mencher, Melvin. Basic News Writing. New Delhi: Brown Publishers, 1990. Print.
9. Wardhaugh, Ronald. An Introduction to Sociolinguistics. Oxford: Blackwell, 1998. Print.
10. Melin, Tracy L., and Nina Ray. "Emphasizing Foreign Language Use to International Marketing Students: A Situational Exercise That Mimics Real-World Challenges." Global Business Languages 10 (2005): 13-25. Print.
11. Vestergard, Torben, and Kim Schrorder. The Language of Advertising. New York: Basil Blackwell, 1985. Print.
12. 黄国文. 语篇分析的理论与实践：广告语篇研究. 上海：上海外语教育出版社，2001
13. 王军元. 广告语言. 上海：汉语大词典出版社，2005
14. 王睿. "团购还是"坑"团?" 家用电脑08 (2011): 1. Web. 16 May 2012. http:// ep.cbifamily.com/2011/08/5/134453.html
15. 京东网. 360Buy 京东商城, 2004. Web. 16 May 2012. www.360buy.com
16. 淘宝网. 阿里巴巴集团,2003.Web. 16 May 2012. www.taobao.com
17. 阿里巴巴. 阿里巴巴集团,1999.Web. 16 May 2012. http://china.alibaba.com/
18. 凡客诚品网.VANCL凡客诚品, 2007. Web. 16 May 2012. www.vancl.com
19. 当当网. n.p., 2004. Web. 16 May 2012. www.dangdang.com
20. 亚马逊.Amazon.com Inc., 1999. Web. 16 May 2012. www.amazon.cn
21. 新蛋网. 新蛋集团, 2001. Web. 16 May 2012. www.newegg.com.cn
22. 麦考林. 上海麦考林信息集团有限公司, 2000. Web. 16 May 2012. www.m18.com
23. 新浪网新闻中心. SINA Cooperation, 1996. Web. 16 May 2012. http://news.sina.com.cn/c/2011-12-26/223523698693.shtml
24. 赛迪网新闻中心. 赛迪集团, 2000. Web. 16 May 2012. http://news.ccidnet.com/art/11097/20111230/3490499_1.html
25. HZ深圳会展指南. n.p. Web. 16 May 2012.
26. 网中网. n.p., 2009. Web. 16 May 2012. http://www.wtoow.com/new/20120110/35860846.html
27. 南信校园论坛. 南京信息职业技术学院,2001. Web. 16 May 2012. http://bbs.njcit.cn/thread-38560-1-1.html
28. 凤凰网.凤凰新媒体, 2011. Web. 16 May 2012. http://news.ifeng.com/society/2/detail_2011_07/17/7744750_0.shtml
29. 天极网笔记本电脑频道. 天极传媒, 1999.Web. 16 May 2012.
30. 中国新闻网. 中国新闻社, 1995. Web. 16 May 2012. http://www.chinanews.com/yl/2012-01-16/3608432.shtml
31. 良无限.Taobao.com, 2003. Web. 16 May 2012. http://lp.taobao.com/go/act/sale/lxw_index.php
32. 瑞丽美容网. 瑞丽传媒, 2001. Web. 16 May 2012. http://beauty.rayli.com.cn/bodycare/2012-05-15/L0003018003_957094.html
33. Only Lady 女人志. Only Lady, 1996. Web. 16 May 2012. http://bbs.onlylady.com/read-htm-tid-2900585.html
34. 凤凰博报. 凤凰新媒体, 2011. Web. 16 May 2012. http://blog.ifeng.com/article/11502528.html
35. 龙虎网. 龙虎网络传播有限公司, 2002. Web. 16 May 2012.

http://news.longhoo.net/

36. 名品导购网. 上海中主信息科技有限公司, 2004.Web. 16 May 2012.
    http://www.mplife.com/

37. 购物女小炜炜卡骆驰Crocs淘宝旗舰店 .Taobao.com, 2012. Web. 16 May 2012.
    http://shop35754389.taobao.com/

38. 腾讯拍拍网. 腾讯公司 , 1998. Web. 16 May 2012. http://paipai.com/

39. 助购网美容频道.n.p., 2006. Web. 16 May 2012. http://beauty.zhugou.com

40. 百度知道. Baidu Inc., 2012. Web. 16 May 2012.
    http://zhidao.baidu.com/question/83427907

41. 百度百科.Baidu Inc., 2012. Web. 16 May 2012.
    http://baike.baidu.com/view/2724065.htm

42. 百度. Baidu Inc., 2007. Web. 16 May 2012
    http://hi.baidu.com/hujingjian/blog/item/312c564e67a61c0bb2de051e.html

43. IT 时代周刊.IT 时代周刊,2003. Web. 16 May 2012.
    http://www.ittime.com.cn/index.php?m=content&c=index&a=show&catid=56&id=436

44. 合肥购物网. 合肥热线 , 2003. 16 May 2012. http://gouwu.hefei.cc/

45. 新浪视频. 新浪公司,2011.Web. 16 May 2012.
    http://video.sina.com.cn/p/ent/v/2011-08-12/144861443235.html

---

Hong Li, Ph.D. teaches Chinese language and culture at Emory University in the Department of Russian and East Asian Languages and Cultures.   Shan-shan Wang is a visiting faculty member at the Confucius Institute at Georgia State University.

Hong Kong and Macau: Two Dynamos in China's Pearl River Delta

Clifton W. Pannell

Vol. 10, No.2
2011

In the waning days of their colonial existence, Hong Kong and Macau were like mismatched cousins. Hong Kong was a roaring entrepôt of commerce while Macau was a sleepy backwater sustained mainly by gambling. Fourteen years after Hong Kong was handed back to China, and 12 years after Macau returned to Chinese sovereignty, the cousins are starting to look very different. Hong Kong is still holding its own as a dynamic industrial and financial center. But Macau has blossomed, becoming in many ways unrecognizable.

In this paper, I seek to offer a brief explanation of the development of the two regions since the handover and explore some of the challenges each has experienced in the search for new and productive roles as Special Administrative Regions within the PRC. This search has provided an urgent impetus for both cities not only to identify and follow an appropriate and effective track on which to return to China, but more immediately to seek the appropriate role for their evolving integration into what has emerged as one of China's most dynamic city-regions - the Pearl River Delta (PRD).

Today the PRD, if we include the more than 7 million people in Hong Kong and the more than half-a-million in Macau, comprises a booming city-region with a population of more than 50 million. Its economic output and linkage to the global economy puts it at the leading edge of China's remarkable economic growth. We estimate its contribution to China's gross domestic product as roughly 10% of the nation's total output.

Hong Kong and Macau are located on the east and west flanks respectively of China's Pearl River Delta. (Fig. 1) They are located at what may be viewed as the feet of two legs of a triangle with Guangzhou (Canton) at the head. These are three of the core cities of the booming city-region surrounding the estuary of the Pearl River in southeastern China's Guangdong Province.

Both cities share a European colonial heritage, but they are remarkably different in size, historical role and development, and economic trajectory. Hong Kong was returned to Chinese sovereignty in July, 1997; Macau followed two years later in December, 1999. Upon their return, both cities were awarded status as Special Administrative Regions (SAR). Their status as SARs, governed by a "Basic Law," similar to a constitution, has allowed each to have 50 years of separate and semi-autonomous development within the larger context of being a legal part of China.

Fig. 1. Pearl River Delta showing location of Hong Kong and Macau. Courtesy: Mapsof.net

Hong Kong's colonial development began in 1842 following the Opium War and Britain's desire for a commercial beachhead and deep port to advance its ambitions for the China trade. Initially limited to Hong Kong Island and a small piece of the Kowloon Peninsula, later treaties added offshore islands and the New Territories. Its growth and development progressed dynamically, although sometimes erratically, thereafter. Hong Kong's role as gateway and sentinel for the China trade was rapidly propelled following the establishment of the People's Republic of China (PRC) in 1949 and new China's efforts to end the extensive commercial activities of Shanghai and other treaty ports along China's coast. Once adjacent locations such as Zhuhai and Shenzhen were designated as Special Economic Zones (SEZ) in the early 1980s when China began its serious economic reforms, Hong Kong's role as a source of capital, commercial knowledge and knowhow, and ties to the world economic system were crucial to China's modernization efforts. These were greatly intensified after the two southern trips of paramount leader Deng Xiaoping in the early 1990s. Hong Kong has indeed been the tip of the commercial spear for China's extraordinary economic development of the last 30 years.

Macau was first established in 1557 as a tiny port and residential center for Portuguese traders who periodically visited the trade fairs in Canton (Guangzhou). The Chinese allowed them to stay there, although they exercised no sovereignty over the territory for more than three centuries. As was typical of both Portuguese and Spanish colonial efforts, Catholic missionaries soon followed, and Macau became a center for the activities for the Jesuits in East Asia. Throughout much of its history, Macau has struggled for financial resources to support itself. Traditional forms of Chinese gambling were tolerated early, and eventually these became a source of revenue. Hong Kong's rise undermined the port and trading functions of Macau, and after 1842 Macau quickly became a stagnant backwater for a century-and-a-half. In 1962 a gambling monopoly was established with improved casinos and hotels; gambling was taxed and became an important source of revenue. At the same time, crime flourished and Macau developed a seedy reputation for its smoky and rough gambling casinos. Following the handover to China in 1999, the monopoly was ended and modern Las Vegas-style casinos were invited to share in the development of a new Macau. This has led to new prosperity and a transformation Macau has never before witnessed.

Hong Kong and its recent path

In the 21st Century Hong Kong faces a number of challenges, and many emanate from the adjacent booming industrial and port cities next door, such as Shenzhen and Dongguan. What has happened since the Chinese economic reforms of the late 1970s, and more rapidly since Deng Xiaoping's southern trip in 1992 where he implored China's citizens that to get rich was glorious, is an explosion in the economic development of the Pearl River Delta. Manufacturing migrated from Hong Kong to the PRD where the costs of land, construction, waste removal and especially labor were much less expensive than in Hong Kong. Over three decades the PRD became the factory engine of China for many consumer products that were then re-exported through Hong Kong and more recently shipped directly from the PRD through container ports such as those attached to Shenzhen.

Hong Kong has continued to prosper as it retained the headquarters role with management, finance, marketing and research and development functions of industrial enterprises still based there. The model became front office (Hong Kong) and rear factory (Dongguan and Shenzhen in the PRD). The port of Hong Kong with its very modern container facilities burgeoned initially and became the world's largest at the turn of the century. In recent years, this function has slipped relatively as Shanghai, Singapore and Shenzhen have enlarged their container shipping facilities and operations. Shenzhen, immediately adjacent to Hong Kong, is a serious rival, as its labor, port handling and transfer costs are lower than Hong Kong's, and it continues to improve the quality of its customer services. Hong Kong's shipping functions, while continuing to be very important to its economy, nevertheless are gradually diminishing, as their neighboring competitors ramp up their operations and efficiencies.

Other key aspects of Hong Kong's economy such as banking and finance, commercial services, tourism and retail continue to flourish, but they too are facing new challenges. While Hong Kong traditionally has been a key center for capital accumulation and the transfer of foreign direct investment into the Pearl River region, China today has accumulated huge foreign reserves and its dependence on Hong Kong to lead the way into linkages with the global economy has declined. Hong Kong's role as a key banking and finance center remains in the lead, but again as China increasingly embeds itself in the global financial system, Hong Kong must move nimbly to ensure it has a role as interlocutor and middleman, providing negotiating skills and a vast array of brokerage services between China and other global economic powers. This role was crucial for China's economic success in the 1980s and 1990s, but the maturing and expanding of economic reforms throughout China have reduced the importance of this need for Hong Kong's intercession.

Among Hong Kong's challenges are the issues of its continuing democratic institutions as well as the social welfare of all its citizens. While its 50 years of separate development allow for the continuation of free elections and determining its own governance structure and processes, the shadow of mainland China always looms, and the extent of Hong Kong autonomy has never been entirely clear. At the same time enormous wealth has been created. There are many extremely rich people, yet there is also a substantial number of low-income people, and the distribution of wealth is very uneven. Hong Kong people see themselves as somewhat different from their mainland cousins, nevertheless their destinies are closely intertwined and mutually dependent. It seems clear that Hong Kongers must increasingly accept the reality of their gradual reintegration into China while working diligently to ensure it is a productive reintegration.

Yet Hong Kong has many special and distinctive attributes that indicate it will continue to play a special role in China's future. For example, it has placed increasing emphasis and investment in higher education through funding and expansion of its universities. This has included increasing stress on technical areas such as medicine, engineering, science and research. Many more students from the China mainland are coming to Hong Kong, and the Times of London Higher Education Supplement has given very high marks to some of the universities such as the University of Hong Kong for the quality of its programs, faculty, students and its research productivity. In this role Hong Kong, with its emphasis on the continued use of the English language as an international medium of communication for education, business, science and culture has been successful in maintaining a special role both within the Pearl River Delta Region as well as within the broader framework of developing China.

Macau's Amazing Ascent

Hong Kong's story of growth and expansion as a British colony and its subsequent return to China is oft told and well-known. Among the most frequently discussed topics about Hong Kong is how it has fared under Chinese sovereignty. Macau's is, in many ways, a much more intriguing and dramatic tale, especially since its return to the motherland. Ever since the establishment of Hong Kong around 1840, Macau has suffered from the presence of its larger neighbor. Small, and with a shallow harbor that was increasingly silted up, Macau formally came under Portuguese sovereignty in 1888, after almost three-and-a-half centuries of legal ambiguity about its status as way station for Portuguese and other foreign traders seeking entry to the Canton trading fairs. During Hong Kong's rise, Macau became a poor backwater with a limited economic base, always searching for some way to make money and support itself. Gambling in dirty, dimly lit gaming houses and other sometimes nefarious activities resulted, and over time the territory earned a seedy reputation.

Some improvements in the quality of gambling houses led to a few casinos after the appointment of a monopoly in 1962 to the Sociedade de Tourismo e Diversoes de Macau (Macau Tourist and Amusement Company) which introduced some of the western gambling games and provided new monies to improve infrastructure in the harbor and ferry landings. Yet during the last years of Portuguese rule, organized crime flourished, and the power of Chinese Triads grew. That led to shootings in the casinos and on the streets. After China took over in 1999, a more effective local administration quickly put a stop to the open crime and moved to improve the gambling scene. The STDM monopoly was ended, and new licenses were awarded in 2002 to a successor of the STDM as well as to two Western syndicates, Galaxy and Wynn, with the goal of expanding and modernizing the casino/gaming scene based on the Las Vegas model. Growing the gaming (now the preferred terminology for gambling, with gamblers now called "players") industry in this way would also lead to increased fiscal resources and an attendant increase in public funding to develop Macau's infrastructure and social services.

The results have been astounding! With the introduction of the new casinos and hotels, tourist visits surged, and the casinos were doing a bumper business. Gross gaming revenues also accelerated. From 2003 to 2008 the gross gaming revenue increased four-fold, rising from $3.6 billion to $13.7 billion; gaming revenues surpassed those of Las Vegas in 2006. This number exceeded the combined revenue of all the casinos in Las Vegas and Atlantic City by 2008 and established

Macau as the leading gaming city in the world. In 2010, Macau's gross gaming revenues hit $23.5 billion, and the monthly revenue from February to May 2011 has grown by at least 42% (Table 1).

Table 1: Comparative Casino Revenue: Macau, Las Vegas, and Singapore, 2010	
Macau:	$23.5 Billion
Las Vegas:	$5.8 Billion
Singapore:	$5.1 Billion
Source: Loughlin and Pannell, 2010; The Associated Press, 2011	

Perhaps the most striking transformation is in the cityscape. New casinos and hotels are springing up, especially in the area called Cotai, a place created with landfill between the two islands of Taipa and Coloane that sit south of the Macau peninsula (Fig.2).

New roads, causeways and bridges link this new area with its grand hotels and casinos - Venetian, Galaxy, Hard Rock and others - to the Macau peninsula where a number of new casino/hotel complexes also have appeared around the Grand Lisboa and Wynn Macau. The annual number of visitors also has increased dramatically and exceeded 21 million in 2009. This number may

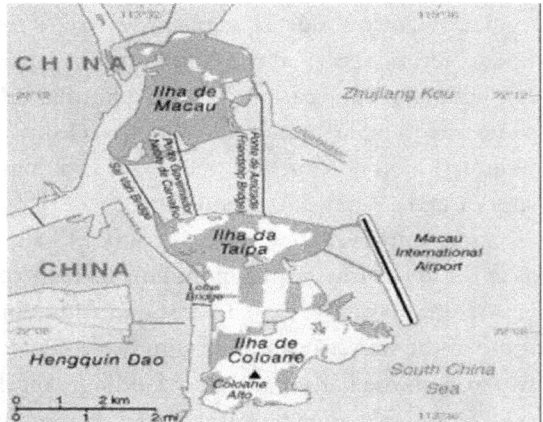

Fig. 2. Macau. Area between Ilha da Taipa and Ilha de Coloane is Cotai landfill area on which are located many of the new casinos.

someday reach the number of tourists in Hong Kong, a much larger and better known place. Yet these tourists are different. Many of them are day-trippers or stay only one night. The visitors to Hong Kong usually stay at least three nights. They come to Macau primarily to gamble. Shopping, sightseeing and other recreational pursuits are low on the list of things to do. Most Macau visitors are also from China, and many literally walk into the SAR from nearby Zhuhai, as they pass through the China Gate where buses from the casinos will meet them and whisk them directly to a casino of their choice.

Macau has never witnessed anything like what is happening today during its 450 years of colonial history. This new, unprecedented wealth and prosperity have changed this one-time backwater to the most favored spot in Asia and perhaps the world for those who wish to try their luck at roulette, baccarat, blackjack or a traditional Chinese game such as Sic Bo or even the old favorite of Fan Tan. A fiscal policy that imposed a gambling tax of 35% of gross casino revenue has provided the SAR with more than 75% of its overall revenues and allowed it to greatly upgrade infrastructure and increase the support of social services for the residents while keeping other taxes low.

While the new wealth and prosperity have done many good things for Macau, there are also questions as to the social costs of gambling. Given that most of the gamblers come from China and Hong Kong, however, these costs are not likely to show up in Macau, but issues such as seriously addicted gamblers do not disappear, and the costs must be borne somewhere. Another emerging issue resulting from Macau's new wealth is ensuring all citizens benefit. Improved social welfare programs and educational opportunities offer new prospects, but these must be comprehensive and sustained if they are to succeed. Meanwhile, the good times are rolling in Macau. Gambling is forbidden in mainland China, and the future looks very bright for continued growth in gaming and Macau's related prosperity. While other competitors have recently emerged in Singapore, Taiwan, Philippines and Korea, Macau has established its reputation as the world's premier gaming center, and its challengers can only marvel at its success.

Today Hong Kong and Macau are both in the process of establishing their revised identities as Special Administrative Regions of China. Their colonial heritage and historical evolution give them a distinct character that offers both promise and challenge. Hong Kong's role has been primarily commercial, and it was very important during the first three decades of economic reform in China. Today Hong Kong is expanding its role and identity as a global financial, commercial and educational center for southeast China and is a world city offering leadership for its neighbors in the Pearl River Delta region as they strive to integrate more closely with the global economy.

Macau by contrast muddled along until after the handover in 1999. Its new identity has become that of China's leading recreational and tourist center for gambling. So successful has this been that Macau has emerged as the world's greatest and most advanced gaming center when measured by revenue turnover. The last decade has brought remarkable new prosperity but also new challenges in maintaining its distinctive and special character. It seems China is satisfied with the evolving role of both places and the gradual shifts in their functions and character as they renew their ties and establish their revised identities under the motherland.

References and Bibliography:

The Associated Press, 2011, as reported in the AJC June 7, "Singapore to take No. 2 gambling spot from Vegas," http://www.ajc.com/travel/singapore-to-take-no-969644.html?printArticle=y.

Bradsher, K. 2010. Hong Kong moves ahead on reforms. New York Times. June 21. http://www.

netimes.com/2010/06/22world/asia/22hongkong.html?-r=1&ref=asia.

The Economist,(2011, Feb. 12). Development in China: The Pearl River mega-city, http://www. economist.com/blogs/gulliver/2011/02development_china

GHK (Hong Kong) Ltd. (2008) Executive Summary. Study on Hong Kong Port Forecasts - Master Plan, 2005/2006.

Healy, Tim (2004) "Big gamblers bet on Macau," Wall Street Journal. March 5.

International Herald Tribune, (2006). "A $1 billion bet on Macao as the Las Vegas of the East." September 5.

Lin, George C.S., (2010) The Pearl River Delta in A New Geography of Hong Kong, eds. C. Y. Jim, Li Si Ming, and Fung Tung, Vol. 2. Cosmos Books, Hong Kong.

Lin, George C.S., (1997) Red Capitalism in South China: Growth and Development of the Pearl River Delta. University of British Columbia Press. Vancouver, B.C.

Loughlin, Philip H. and Clifton W. Pannell, (2010) "The port of Hong Kong: Past successes, new realities, and emerging challenges," Focus on Geography. Vol 53, No. 2.

Loughlin, Philip H. and Clifton W. Pannell, (2010) "Gambling in Macau: A brief history and glance at today's modern casinos," Focus on Geography. Vol . 53, No. 1.

Mapsof.net, 2011. http://mapsof.net/map/pearl-river-delta-area.

Porter, Jonathan, 1996. Macau, the imaginary city: culture and society. Westview Press, Boulder, CO.

The Times Higher Education World University Rankings, 2010-2011 http://www.timeshighereducation.co.uk/world-university-rankings/2010-2011/top-200.html.

Wan, Y.K.P., Li, X., and Kong, W. H. (in press), "The social impacts of casino gaming in Macao," Tourism: An International Interdisciplinary Journal.

Wang, James J. and Michael C. Cheng (2010). "From a hub port city to a global supply chain management center: a case study of Hong Kong" Journal of Transport Geography. Vol 18.

Yee, Herbert S. (2001) Macau in Transition: From colony to Autonomous Region. Palgrave, Basingtoke, UK.

Clifton W. Pannell, Ph.D. is emeritus faculty in the Department of Geography, University of Georgia.

Soft Landings Curriculum for U.S.-China Entrepreneurship

Ye-Sho Chen, Edward Watson, and Renato Ferreira Leitão Azevedo

Vol.10, No.2
2011

Introduction

The soft landings program developed originally by the National Business Incubation Association (NBIA 2011) was designed to help a company from one country land softly into the market of another country through a local incubator.[1] The purpose of the program is to help reduce risks and costs for the company as well as to find business opportunities in the new market. There are two key success factors in the soft landings program: (1) connecting the expanding company with key decision-makers from relevant network supply chain companies in the new market and (2) providing revenue generation services for the company (Mencin and Erikson 2009). A major driver behind the two key success factors is global talent retention and recruiting (Hansen et al. 2000; McLean and McLean 2001; Beebe, et al. 2006).

The objective of the Soft Landings Curriculum (SLC) (Chen et al. 2010; Liu et al. 2010) is to provide a curricular platform for cultivating talented people for the expanding companies by linking college students at various levels (e.g., undergraduate, graduate and executive education) with business communities engaging in the soft landings program. The SLC enables the company to reduce risks and costs, find business opportunities and identify talented people for its new business-venture. Moreover, the participating students are able to (1) network

1   Acknowledgement: *The paper was the research result of a grant from the Business and International Education of U.S. Department of Education, entitled "Cultivating Global Entrepreneurs through U.S.-China Business Education at Louisiana State University." The authors would like to express their sincere thanks for the support.*

with key decision makers at both the expanding company and the supply chain companies; (2) engage in developing revenue generation models for the expanding company; (3) earn income or internships; (4) become employees or partners of the expanding company and (5) create their own businesses by leveraging the networked resources developed in the course of participation. The SLC program achieves a win-win situation for everyone involved.

In this paper we discuss how the SLC works at LSU. Silberman (2006, p.158-159) raises several questions that should be taken into account when shaping and designing active learning experiences: (1) Does the design achieve the activity's objective? (2) What knowledge or skill level does the design require of participants? (3) How much time will it take? (4) Is the design slow or fast-paced? (5) Is it suited to the size of the group? (6) What skills are required to conduct the design? With that in mind specifically, we answer the following eight questions with the goal that the lessons learned at LSU could be a real aid for those who might want to set up a similar approach at their own universities.

- What components are necessary for developing an SLC?
- How do we develop an SLC?
- What do the students do from week to week and how do their activities tie into social networking and linking up with local incubators and Chinese student partners?
- How do the students get from making contacts with Chinese students to doing actual projects with real companies?
- How is a trip to China organized and how is it funded?
- At what point do the students develop their business plans?
- Are case studies available that describe these success stories?
- What kinds of area resources are essential in making this kind of course a success?

1. What components are necessary for developing an SLC?

There are three major components of an SLC: first, companies interested in expanding their businesses into other countries; second, local incubators available to assist in the expansion and third, curricular programs allowing students to help companies land softly into local incubators. In this section, we discuss how we start on these three components.

Companies Interested in Soft Landings to Expand Their Business

In their book on how China's cost innovation is changing global competition, Zeng and Williamson (2007) identify the evolution of foreign multinationals' business relationship with China in the following four stages: (1) made in China, using China to manufacture their products for the global markets; (2) market in China, selling products to the rising domestic market in China; (3) innovation in China, investing in R&D, design, and branding to innovate and lead in China and (4) global brands from China, selling products globally that were originated and successfully marketed in China. Industries on the frontier of this evolution include textile and apparel, shoes, toys, consumer electronics, home appliances and personal computers. The need to transform from Made-in-China to Global-Brands-from-China is discussed in Harney's book on China Price (2008), in which she argues China is losing its cost advantage. With the recent endorsement of China's 12th Five-Year Plan (2011-2015), we see a clearer plan for this transformation, especially regarding the Chinese market and Chinese innovation (KPMG 2011).

The transformation of China's economy means increased opportunities for U.S.-China entrepreneurship. In particular, there will be more U.S. companies in need of soft landings into the China market and more Chinese companies in need of soft landings into the U.S. market. There are various ways to engage with these companies. Here are some of our examples:

- Through the networks of the International Franchise Forum, a component of Stephenson Entrepreneurship Institute at LSU, we have received soft landings requests from several U.S.-based franchise companies interested in the growing consumer markets in China (KPMG 2011).
- Through the networks of our partners in China, we have received the soft landings requests from several Chinese companies interested in the U.S. markets, e.g., clean energy and senior care.
- Through our alumni networks we have received the soft landings requests from U.S.-to-China and China-to-U.S. companies. For example, an EMBA alumnus, who is a physician, is interested in the market opportunities of health care in China (KPMG 2011). Another example, a student from China is interested in expanding his family business into the U.S.

Local Incubators Available to Assist Soft Landings

Local incubators for soft landings are those having the capacity of helping foreign companies develop their new local markets through their incubators. Consider, as an example, Louisiana Business and Technology Center (LBTC), a local incubator at LSU. In operation since 1988, LBTC was selected as the 2005 Technology Incubator of the Year by the National Business Incubation Association. In 2006, LBTC won the Excalibur Award from the Association of University Research Parks for its leadership in housing numerous technology companies displaced by hurricanes during the post-Katrina and Rita periods. More significantly, LBTC's mobile classroom program received the 2009 Excellence in Rural Economic Development award by the U.S. Economic Development Administration.

LBTC's capacity of helping companies develop new markets consists of three pillars:

- Business incubation: These services include facilities, management and technical assistance, financial analysis, access to capital, referral to fee-based professional and advisor resources, technology transfer and commercialization assistance and entrepreneurial educational training.
- Business counseling and networking: These services include seminars and workshops on current practices and changing trends, providing networking opportunities to gain resources, providing access to resources and expertise within the federal laboratory system, outreach to rural communities in Louisiana through the mobile classroom, business emergency operations and providing a key link between LSU and business communities for joint venture exploration and program development in the U.S. and China.
- Talent cultivation and recruiting: LBTC's regional, national and international resources and networks provide fertile ground to cultivate talents for expanding companies. Consider three examples. First, MBA students with qualified skills work as business development counselor assistants at LBTC. Second, LBTC works closely with LSU's Stephenson Entrepreneurship Institute's Entrepreneurship Fellow Program to provide students the opportunity to network with and be mentored by top executives. It thereby gives these students an extra edge in developing their business plans. Third, LBTC provides a Student Incubator to help students develop and advance their business plans.

Curriculum Designed to Help Foreign Companies to Land Softly

Based on the literature review, a meaningful SLC shall cultivate talents (Hansen et al. 2000; McLean and McLean 2001; Beebe, et al. 2006) who can help soft landings companies get connected with key decision-makers within the supply chain in the new market and provide revenue generation services for the soft landings company (Mencin and Erikson 2009).

An SLC can be interpreted as a strategy for instruction leading to learning. According to Smith and Ragan (2005) instructional design "refers to the systematic and reflective process of translating principles of learning and instruction into plans for instructional materials, activities, information resources and evaluation." Considering their concepts for design and instruction, it is possible to rephrase, saying that instructional design is the field responsible for the process, activities and people engaged to improve the quality of their subsequent creations in order to develop and deliver information and outputs that are created to facilitate attainment of intended and specific learning goals. Based on the process involved, instructional design is divided into three major activities, which are to perform an instructional analysis, to develop an instructional strategy and to develop and conduct an evaluation. The first activity aims to answer, "Where we are going?," the second, "How we will get there?" and the third "How we will know when we are there?" The instructional design structure is based on learning that meets learners' needs.

- With this background of instructional design in mind, we have developed a five-step SLC:
- Step 1: Develop social networking opportunities for LSU students to learn the needs of U.S. decision-makers interested in doing business in China as well as Chinese decision-makers interested in doing business in the U.S.
- Step 2: Develop a social media platform, such as Twitter, Facebook or Skype, for U.S. students to communicate with Chinese students at partnering universities and explore solutions to the needs identified in the first step.
- Step 3: Develop student mobility for students to visit and network with the decision-makers in the U.S.-China supply chains related to the solutions explored in the second step.
- Step 4: Assist students to develop robust business plans.
- Step 5: Work with our soft landings clients and student ambassadors to build their businesses in the U.S. or China utilizing the local incubators.

Due to the effects of the recession on higher education, we realized at the outset in Spring 2007 that in order for the SLC program to be sustainable, we needed to be self-sufficient. Fortunately, we have been graced with collaborative partners who are willing to share resources and move the SLC program forward. Specifically, in collaboration with partners in China, this action-oriented SLC program is the concerted effort of the following entities at LSU:

1. The Emerging Markets Initiative: The Initiative has developed courses and resources for doing business with emerging markets.
2. The Flores MBA Program: The Program, ranked 31st in 2010 by Forbes, provides the linkages to business communities, including the development of soft landings curricula for full-time, part-time and executive MBA students. The Program also organizes business trips to emerging markets.
3. The Stephenson Entrepreneurship Institute: The outstanding success of SEI allowed LSU to be ranked 3rd as America's most entrepreneurial campus by the Princeton Review and Forbes in 2004. SEI organizes seminars and provides business plan development advice.
4. The Louisiana Business Technology Center: The Center, designated the 2005 Technology Incubator of the Year, provides incubating facilities that assure the successful implementation of business plans developed by soft landings participants. The LSU business incubator also provides

space and services to companies from emerging markets or joint ventures with U.S. firms to give them a starting place in which to develop their businesses in U.S.

5. The International Programs at LSU: The Programs leverage the network resources of LSU international students from emerging markets. The Programs also provide the linkages to international business programs around the world.

2. How Do We Develop the SLC?

To move the SLC program forward, we have developed a rich repository of resources and networks focused on U.S.-China business education and entrepreneurship. The resources include a knowledge repository of courses and cases on U.S.-China business opportunities. Consider, for example, the following three courses:

- Sourcing in China: Sourcing plays a vital role in global business competition. Understanding how sourcing in China works and doesn't work is critical for firms seeking to thrive in the 21st century. Students take this course to understand the general characteristics behind the successes and failures of sourcing in China and show what firms can learn to succeed in executing their sourcing strategies. The students will explore opportunities of helping U.S. companies choose strategic partners and suppliers in China.

- Entrepreneurship in China: Entrepreneurship plays a vital role in modern Chinese business. Understanding how Chinese entrepreneurs thrive is critical for foreign firms seeking to grow in China. Students take this course to understand the general characteristics behind successful Chinese entrepreneurs and to show what foreign firms can learn from them to thrive in China.

- Emerging Markets and Supply Chain Opportunities: The rise of emerging markets, such as China, India and Brazil, produces various entrepreneurial opportunities in global supply chains. This course seeks to understand the general characteristics behind successful business cases in retail global supply chain, product life cycle and global supply chain, supplier clusters and emerging markets, information technology and global supply chain, life-saving supply chain and disaster management, and greening the global supply chain. The students explore entrepreneurial opportunities for local communities playing the role of growing the U.S. economy.

U.S.-China business education and entrepreneurship networks include key decision -makers of U.S.-China businesses, success storytellers and their networks.

The networks are developed from various sources, including LSU international alumni networks, Chinese faculty, LSU students from China, members of the globalization committee in the Dean's Advisory Board, the Louisiana Business & Technology Center, the Baton Rouge Area Chamber of Commerce, the Baton Rouge Center for World Affairs, Social Entrepreneurs of New Orleans, the Louisiana Cultural Economy and World Cultural Economic Forum, the Port of New Orleans and the World Trade Center in New Orleans.

3. What Do the Students Do?

The first step of the SLC process is to develop social networking opportunities for LSU students to learn the needs of U.S. decision-makers interested in doing business in China as well as Chinese decision-makers interested in doing business in the U.S. In this section, we discuss what students do from week to week and how their activities tie into social networking, linking up with local incubators and Chinese student partners.

Social Networking

Three effective networking approaches for students to learn the needs of decision-makers are the following:

- Invite interested decision-makers to speak at related classes, such as Sourcing in China and Entrepreneurship in China, to discuss what they need and what incentives they can offer for inspired students to pursue further to the next steps.
- Invite success storytellers as speakers to inspire the students about their journeys and connect the students to their networks.
- Hold seminars and workshops on Doing Business with China for students, faculty and Louisiana business communities. They provide opportunities, such as internships, for students to network with business people.

Consider, for examples, the needs of U.S. franchises interested in doing business in China. There are three general needs. The first need is to help them establish the company headquarters in China through trustful Chinese partners in legal, site selection, human resources, supply chain and marketing. The second need is to help them develop the franchise strategy to grow the business, including standard operation procedures for franchised units and franchisee selection. The third need is to help them with product R&D. The Chinese market is highly competitive and intellectual property protections are relatively loose. A common strategy to address the two issues is to constantly develop new products Chinese consumers like.

As for Chinese decision-makers interested in doing business with U.S., here are some examples:

- A growing natural medicine company in Beijing. The company has R&D, manufacturing facilities and a hospital focused on natural medicine. The company is growing into the vertical market in natural medicine in China by mergers and acquisitions and purchasing land for growing herbs found in natural medicine. Seeing the demand of natural medicine among the increased population of retired baby boomers in the U.S., a senior executive of the company visited LSU for six months in 2010 to develop collaborative projects with the teams, including faculty and students, at LSU.

- leading jeans manufacturer in China. The owner has much knowledge and a strong network in the textile industry in China. By leveraging networked resources, the company has developed a new fashion brand ready to go global. The owner visited LSU for three months in Spring 2011 with three objectives: exploring the market opportunities for the new brand, looking for U.S. brands with a rich history to adapt for China markets and exporting good U.S. household brands to China's developing markets.

- A large solar energy component manufacturer in China. The company's raw materials come from a U.S.-based company specializing in turning sand into high quality silicon. The company is interested in expanding into the U.S. market by first finding solar panel installers and distributors here. Once they understand the market demands in U.S., they plan to invest in domestic solar panel manufacturing. It is worth noting that the owner's children are studying at LSU. They are expected to participate in the U.S. venture and eventually become executives of the company's U.S. office.

Week-to-Week Activities

Students inspired by the opportunities presented by the decision-makers of an expanding company may work on a class project, individually or as a team, to fully understand the needs of the company in the new market. The project includes five major questions:

- What are the demand and supply chains of the company in the home country?
- What is the current business model for revenue generation in the home country?
- What are the demand and supply chains of the company in the new market?
- What are potential revenue generation models in the new market through the local incubator?
- How can companies relate the findings from the first four questions to

the specific needs of the decision makers?

The students have to present weekly reports summarizing their activities, findings and questions. They also have to make one mid-term presentation and another final presentation allowing them to learn how to effectively present their findings and gain valuable feedback from the audience, including classmates and the representatives of the soft landings companies. From time to time, Chinese student partners at LSU or in China are introduced to help answer the questions.

4. From Networking to Real Projects

The second step of the SLC process is to develop a social media platform for U.S. students to communicate with Chinese students at partnering universities and explore solutions to the needs identified in the first step. In this section, we discuss how the students get from making contacts with Chinese students to doing actual projects with real companies.

A key feature of the SLC program is that international resources such as Chinese students at LSU, businesses and their networked resources are leveraged to help interested students explore solutions to the needs. For example, consider the natural medicine company in Beijing described above. The interested U.S. students need to first know the company's demand and supply chains in terms of history, management, market shares, etc. The visit of the senior executive at LSU was helpful in providing needed information. However, the serious U.S. students still needed to use all means available, such as social and face-to-face networking in China and LSU, to fully understand the company.

Another question was to explore how the company's natural medicine products can fit U.S. markets. Three markets were identified and analyzed: drug, medicinal foods and over-the-counter health supplements. The medicinal foods market was selected as a good target for the company's U.S. investments. While exploring solutions for the company, other market opportunities were identified. For example, some U.S. entrepreneurs had patented natural medicine products, but did not have manufacturing capacities. Those entrepreneurs were interested in having the Beijing company manufacture their products for the U.S. and China markets. Another example is a senior care franchise in the U.S. interested in the growing senior care market in China. The franchise company was interested in partnering with the Beijing company to venture into China's market.

5. Gaining Experience in China

The third step of the SLC process is to offer students a chance to visit China and network with the decision-makers in the U.S.-China supply chains related to the solutions explored in the second step. In this section, we discuss how the trip is organized and funded.

Trip Organization

The objective of the trip is to allow students to network with decision-makers and fine-tune their drafted solutions with real-life data and facts. Consider, for example, the natural medicine company in Beijing described above. During the senior executive's six months visit at LSU, we were able to meet with the key decision-makers of the U.S. supply chain in the natural medicine industry. The meetings were arranged by our networked partners in U.S. Some participative students found the meetings very valuable. In return for our assistance, the Chinese senior executive arranged for our students and faculty to visit in the summer of 2010 the key supply chain companies in the Chinese natural medicine industry. The visits include (1) the city Anguo in Hebei, China, famous for its herbal medicines; (2) a top science park where leading natural medicine R&D projects are developed; (3) the company's manufacturing facilities in Beijing, where we found that some of their sophisticated machineries were made in the U.S.; (4) the company's hospital in Beijing, where we saw lengthy processes for treating chronic diseases using Chinese acupuncture; (5) a U.S. company manufacturing capsules in China for the world market; (6) a large pharmaceutical logistics distribution company, where we saw highly automated processes handling the inventory and distribution of the products and (7) a large natural medicine museum, where we saw how Chinese herbal medicine was developed and modernized. Most importantly, the students were able to meet, discuss and network with the key decision-makers in the vertical market of the natural medicine industry in China.

To make the trips to China fruitful, three types of preparations are needed by participants. Consider, for example, the LSU MBA study trip to China. First, we conduct a pre-trip seminar, focusing on linguistic, social and cultural aspects of China. The students are also required to read one or more books, such as China Shakes the World (Kynge 2007), and write a report before the trip. Second is the Doing Business in China group study journal. All students are involved in documenting their study trip experience in a group effort to include narrative and photos. Each group is assigned one of the following five topics discussed in The China Rules (Paine 2010): Dealing with Government, Managing Business Conduct, Developing the Workforce, Competing for Customers and Markets, and Coping with Complexity. The group members are responsible for answering the sub-questions associated with each topic for each company visited.

In addition to the assigned topic, each group will be responsible for summarizing the specific learning that occurred during each day (including site visits, events, seminars or business meetings). Third is the group presentation, summarizing what they have learned during the trip and what they plan to do next. In addition, pictures from the trip will be used to help prepare a Shutterfly.com documentary. This book will be used for promotional purposes targeting both potential MBA prospects as well as potential International Study Trip sponsors. The book will focus on the learning that has occurred during the trip, primarily regarding global business practices but is also reflective of history, culture, geography, politics, law, government and language.

Trip Funding

Typically students have to pay for their own trips. Sometimes we are able to get some financial support from grants or private donations to partially cover travel expenses. For students serious about U.S.-China trade relationships and the opportunities the SLC program can bring, we encourage self-sufficiency. That is, we try to find funding sources from which the findings of their China trips can add value to them. In addition, we prepare trips well so that every fruitful trip may lead to opportunities of another trip funded by someone who can benefit the next time.

6. Developing the Business Plans for Incubation

The fourth step of the SLC process is to help students develop robust business plans. Consider, for example, the leading jeans manufacturer in China and the large solar energy component manufacturer in China described above. Three graduate students and two faculty members were involved in developing the business plan for the jeans company's new brand to market in U.S. The business plan focused on the strategy of using social media to market its products. Two students and one faculty member were involved in developing the business plan for the solar energy company's market in the U.S. The fifth step of SLC is to work with our soft landings clients and student ambassadors to build their businesses in U.S. or China through the local incubators. For example, the solar energy company in China established its U.S. business in March 2010 and incubated at the LSU incubator in January 2011. Through the SLC, the new company was able to reduce risks and costs and recruit talent relatively easily.

7. Impact and Benefits of Cultivating Storytellers

Cultivating Storytellers

The SLC, empowered by the resources and networks such as the foundation, has cultivated storytellers through networking, team building and coaching in every step of companies' soft landings. Below are some examples:

- The Harvard Lady[2]: In a class analyzing the needs of U.S. decision-makers interested in doing business in China, a motivated student was interested in the need of aligning companies' business strategies with the Chinese government's Five-Year plans. Her study led to a research paper, accepted and presented at the Harvard Project for Asian and International Rela-

2   *www.bus.lsu.edu/students/news/stories/2009.03.27_Yuan_Harvard.asp?dept=64*

tions Conference at Harvard University, regarding China's censorship of Google. This success storyteller, The Harvard Lady, became a role model to inspire others to win awards in other competitions.[3]

- The China Lady[4]: In exploring solutions for a Louisiana-based company to do business in China, an inspired student realized the importance of relationship-building and the key role Mandarin plays in the process. She took various Mandarin courses at LSU, attended a study abroad program in China, enrolled in Peking University and maximized the utility of social media to engage in idea discussions with friends in China. Because of her impressive proposal, this student, The China Lady, was hired as an intern in China to evaluate industry opportunities and explore synergies between the company and the Chinese market for possible expansion in the future.

- The Language Man[5]: In networking with U.S.-China supplier chain decision-makers, a gifted student with strong language skills, The Language Man, was able to find a high-paying job in China selling environmental-control products to the global supply chains of multinationals. He also leveraged his supply chain networks to explore a side-business of his own.

- Step 4 - The Who Dat Pig[6]: Inspired by the New Orleans Saints' victory in the Super Bowl and the team's slogan "Who Dat," a highly-connected student partnered with an artistic relative and sourced help in China to quickly turn a class business plan into a real business.

- Step 5 - The Class-On-Demand Man[7]: During the financial crisis in 2008, an entrepreneurial student reflected on the lessons he learned in the Entrepreneurship in China class, specifically the Chinese character for crisis, which is made up of the symbols for danger and opportunity. This student, The Class-On-Demand Man, began to put a business plan together during his final semester at LSU and incorporated many of the ideas taught in class for the future expansion of his business. The business was incubated at the LSU incubator in early 2009. In addition to steadily growing his business, he also incubated another business in late 2010. While enrolled in the class, he got the opportunity to work with several students and business people from China. This real-life experience gave him an understanding of China's market. Seeing the increased number of U.S.-China businesses interested in soft landings through local incubators, he is planning to develop another business to provide online

3   *www.bus.lsu.edu/students/news/stories/2011.03.01_AKP.asp?dept=64*
4   *www.bus.lsu.edu/students/news/stories/2007.11.27_Hicks_China.asp?dept=64*
5   *www.classesondemand.org/videos/CCC_Unsecure/abb8b724867c4be6ac9791d5384fc952*
6   *www.whodatpig.com*
7   *www.bus.lsu.edu/students/news/stories/2009.04.09_Far_East_Student.asp?dept=64*

cross-cultural business etiquette training services for U.S. decision-makers interested in doing business in China and Chinese decision-makers interested in doing business in the U.S.

Impact and Benefits for Instructors, Students, and Other Participants

To successfully conduct business in the global economy, students must acquire international knowledge, including language, business and cultural etiquette, and must have the opportunity for hands-on experience in local markets. Similarly, business communities need to acquire international knowledge and skills for doing business in local markets in order to prepare them to strategically expand their businesses in a global economy. The SLC is designed to take advantage of resources from the participating entities with the impact of enriching our students' educational experience and enabling business communities to engage in global business opportunities. Its significant impact is achieved by:

- Integrating the ongoing efforts of several vibrant entities to enhance awareness of the strategic importance of trade relationships between the U.S. and China, and to promote international business education in Louisiana to cultivate more business-oriented entrepreneurial potential in a global marketplace.
- Bridging the gap between the personnel and information needs of local Louisiana businesses and U.S.-China business education curricula and programs.
- Developing a long-term constructive relationships with academic institutions and the business communities in China to promote international business education and global business in Louisiana in a sustainable manner.

This action-oriented program enhances higher education curriculum and instructional effectiveness by providing the following benefits for instructors, students and other major participants:

- Instructors involved in developing and teaching the SLC: The knowledge accumulated and networked relationships built through the curriculum are documented in a knowledge repository. This will help the instructors teach the curriculum more efficiently and effectively. In addition, the increased number of participating companies in the U.S. and China will be valuable for conducting research toward enhancing the curriculum.
- Students at various levels (undergraduate, graduate, and executive education): In addition to learning real-life business practices in the global context, the curriculum provides the ideal combination of theoretical knowledge, practice and networking opportunities to prepare students to successfully and confidently confront the challenges and opportunities presented by the global marketplace.

- The State of Louisiana: The State of Louisiana, engaging in economic recovery from the damage caused by Hurricanes Katrina and Rita, has a lot to gain from the SLC. State entities focused on business and commerce will benefit immensely through the increased linkages and business opportunities created by the proposed program.
- Louisiana certified minority, women-owned and small businesses in related sectors: The SLC provides a direct link between certified minority, women-owned and small businesses in Louisiana and resources in China. For example, this linkage enables those businesses to gain access to high-quality and low-cost textile/apparel products directly from reputable producers in China. As such, these small businesses will become competitive suppliers for major U.S. fashion manufacturers and retailers.
- U.S. Corporations: Doing more business with certified minority and women-owned businesses in Louisiana adds value to corporate America. Working through the SLC, U.S. corporations can take advantage of some of the best supplier diversity programs through sponsoring LSU students' travel to China.
- Businesses in China interested in going global: Many Chinese apparel manufacturers have competitive advantages of producing high quality products at lower costs than their counterparts in the U.S. These manufacturers are also looking for opportunities to work with the U.S. businesses on establishing their brands to compete in the China market. Business opportunities can be created or facilitated through linking Chinese fashion entrepreneurs with those firms with Louisiana certified minority and women-owned businesses that have extensive knowledge of the U.S. and speak English when presenting products and services to U.S. customers.

8. Essential Area Resources

There are three essential area resources in making the SLC a success:

- A local incubator with a proven track record of success: The incubator plays two major roles: (1) connecting the soft landings company with the key decision-makers from the relevant networked supply chain companies in the local market, and (2) providing revenue generation services for the soft landings company. The example at LSU is the Louisiana Business and Technology Center.
- A U.S.-China business education program: The program plays two major roles: (1) recruiting Chinese companies interested in soft landings in the U.S. and U.S. companies looking to do the same in China, and (2) developing U.S.-China curricula resources to cultivate students' capabili-

ties to engage with soft landings companies. The example at LSU is the Emerging Markets Initiative in the Ourso College of Business.

- An entrepreneurship program with a proven track record of success: The program plays three major roles: (1) cultivating students' entrepreneurial skills; (2) coaching entrepreneurial students to develop business plans to be incubated at the Student Incubator and (3) facilitating the communications between the entrepreneurial students interested in the SLC with the two essential area resources above. The example at LSU is the Stephenson Entrepreneurship Institute in the Ourso College of Business, as well as the Entrepreneurship specialization available to all MBA students.

9. Conclusion

Soft landings is a term from the aviation industry to denote a landing which does not destroy the aircraft. In our work, we use it to refer to a process which helps a company from one country land softly into the market of another country. The E. J. Ourso College of Business at Louisiana State University, in collaboration with business and education partners in China, have developed an action-oriented Soft Landings Curriculum that enables U.S. and Chinese students to explore business opportunities and develop new global ventures by actively helping the Chinese businesses to invest in the U.S. and for U.S. businesses to invest in China. The SLC consists of three basic elements: (1) resources and networks for soft landings as the foundation, (2) five steps of soft landings and (3) cultivating success storytellers through networking, team building and coaching.

In their study of Chinese businesses investing in U.S., Kwan and Sauvant (2008) identified two major challenges: building human resource capacity and navigating overseas political environments. Based on the success of Japanese businesses investing in the U.S., they suggest that Chinese businesses understand the U.S. market and build key relationship within governments and communities and build positive social capital for their companies. The SLC enables the Chinese companies to understand the U.S. market and build key relationships within governments and communities through local incubators in the U.S. The SLC also enables U.S. companies to understand China's market and build key relationships within governments and communities through local incubators in China. By doing so, the costs and risks of investing in U.S. or China are significantly reduced. The SLC also allows the Chinese and U.S. companies to build positive social capital for their businesses by investing in university or college students through a five-step soft landings process. By doing so, the Chinese and U.S. companies are able to cultivate students for talent recruiting and retention to feed growth opportunity. The SLC is a win-win program for everyone involved.

References

Beebe, A., Hew, C., Yueqi, F., and Shi, D., "Going global: Prospects and challenges for Chinese companies on the world stage," IBM Business Consulting Services, IBM Institute for Business Value, March 2006 (www-935.ibm.com/services/us/imc/pdf/g510-6269-going-global.pdf), retrieved in July 2011.

Chen, Y., Watson, E., Liu, C., Cornachione, E., and Wu, S. (2010), "Soft Landings Curriculum of Entrepreneurship in Emerging Markets," Academy of International Business 2010 Annual Meeting, Rio de Janeiro, Brazil, June 25-29.

Hansen, M.T., Chesbrough, H.W., Nohria, N., and Sull, D.N. (2000) "Networked Incubators: Hothouses of the New Economy," Harvard Business Review, September-October, 74-84.

Harney, A. (2008), The China Price: the True Cost of Chinese Competitive Advantage, The Penguin Press.

KPMG (2011), "China's 12th Five-Year Plan (2011-2015)," KPMG Insight Series, (www.kpmg.com/cn/en/IssuesAndInsights/ArticlesPublications/Publicationseries/5-years-plan/Pages/default.aspx), retrieved in July 2011.

Kwan, C. and Sauvant, K.P. (2008), "Chinese Direct Investment in the United States - The Challenges Ahead," Location USA: A Guide for Inward Investment to the Unites States, July (www.locationusa.com/foreignDirectInvestmentUnitedStates/jul08/outward-foreign-direct-investment-china.shtml), retrieved in April 2011.

Kynhe, J. (2007), China Shakes the World, Mariner Books, New York.

Liu, C., Chen, Y., and Belleau, B. (2010), "Soft Landings Curriculum of Fashion Entrepreneurship in Emerging Markets," International Textile and Apparel Association 2010, Montreal, Quebec, Canada, October 27-30.

McLean, G.N. and McLean L. (2001), "If we can't define HRD in one country, how can we define it in an international context?", Human Resource Development International, 4(3): 313 – 326.

Mencin, O. and Erikson, C. (2009) "Silicon Valley's US Market Access Center: The Incubator as a Soft Landings Zone," International Journal of Entrepreneurship and Innovation, Vol. 10, No. 3, 233-241.

NBIA (2011). National Business Incubation Association's Soft Landings Program (www.nbia.org/member_services/soft_landings), retrieved in July 2011.

Paine, L. (2010), "The China Rules," Harvard Business Review, June 1.

Smith, P. L. and Ragan, T. J. (2005), Instructional Design. New York: John Wiley & Sons.

Silberman, M. (2006). Active Training: A handbook of techniques, designs, cases examples, and tips. San Francisco: Pfeiffer.

Zeng, M. and Williamson, P.J. (2007), Dragons at Your Door, Harvard Business School Press.

Ye-Sho Chen, Ph.D. is Director of Emerging Markets Initiative and Edward Watson, Ph.D. is Director of Flores MBA Program, E. J. Ourso College of Business at Louisiana State University, Baton Rouge, Louisiana. Renato Ferreira Leitão Azevedo, MSc. is a Ph.D. Student in the Department of Education Policy, Organization and Leadership at the University of Illinoi, Urbana-Champaign and a Research Fellow at the University of São Paulo, Brazil.

Manufacturing in China: The Key Decisions

An Interview with Scott Ellyson, CEO of East West Manufacturing, Inc.

Vol.10, No.2
2011

Ten years ago, Scott Ellyson and Jeff Sweeney co-founded East West Manufacturing (www.ewmfg.com) in Atlanta to bring U.S.-based companies both the cost-savings and speed-to-market offered by Asian manufacturing, along with the quality control Western companies demand. They began by forging partnerships with a number of manufacturing facilities in China, Thailand, Vietnam, Taiwan and India. Later they purchased factories for their team to operate in Changzhou, China and Ho Chi Minh City, Vietnam. Today, East West Manufacturing is a recognized, respected expert in the planning, design and implementation of offshore product manufacturing for original equipment manufacturers and distributors. The company's transparent supply chain, on-site quality control and logistics systems reduce the risks and complexities of offshore manufacturing.

Scott Ellyson shared his experiences with Penelope Prime, Director of the China Research Center. East-West Manufacturing, Inc. is a sponsor of the Center.

Prime: *You have been working in China for well over a decade. Give us a sense of what has changed and what has stayed fairly consistent in terms of the environment for foreign businesses.*

Ellyson: I made my first trip to China in 1993 and since then have returned more than 100 times. Back then, the sight of a foreigner was so unusual, children would come up to me and touch me. Now, Westerners doing business in China is commonplace. In terms of manufacturing, it's amazing to see the country's transformation in recent years. China has done in 15 years what it would take most countries 50-60 years to accomplish. Their rapid evolution from an agrarian society to an industrial one is remarkable, and makes me wonder what they will accomplish in the next 15 years.

When East West Manufacturing began working in China a decade ago, China's laborers had a well-deserved reputation for their strong work ethic, and the costs of manufacturing were among the lowest in the world. However, the country's poor infrastructure, low-tech suppliers and inexperience with quality control posed difficult challenges. Companies could manufacture products quickly and cheaply in China, but distribution was difficult and product quality was almost never up to U.S. standards.

Let's compare the above scenario with today's business climate. In a remarkably short time, China has built modern freeways, high-speed trains, subway systems and five-star hotels to host business travelers from around the globe. There are high-tech suppliers in place who actively promote their capabilities internationally. While the laborers still work extremely hard, there is a new emphasis on work/life balance. Although the cost-savings of manufacturing in China versus domestic manufacturing are not what they once were, the Chinese have become more adept at managing quality control and they have a greater understanding of the quality demanded by foreign-based companies.

One other striking change is the attitude of the customs agents and other government officials who work with foreign businesspeople. Years ago, they were suspicious, stern and unwelcoming. Today, they are friendly and helpful and make it obvious that they want to encourage our business partnerships. They ask for and act on feedback so they can continue to improve their service and successfully court new business investments.

Prime: Tell us about the early days of setting up your business in China.

Ellyson: Looking back, I'm reminded of how young and idealistic I was. Traveling in China was difficult at every junction. We drove ancient, beat-up Volkswagen Jettas over winding dirt roads full of potholes because there were so few paved roads. We had to constantly zig-zag around pedestrians, cyclists, push carts and livestock. It seems like I was carsick the entire time. I slept on factory floors because there were no hotels nearby. I used to take 30-40 food bars with me because I was unaccustomed to the local food and couldn't tolerate it. I had to spend hours at night feeding documents into a fax machine to communicate with the U.S. and only on rare occasions could I pay for a factory to bring in slow, dial-up internet just so I could send and receive e-mails.

I used to see terrible working conditions in the factories and from the very beginning, we made it clear that if a factory wanted to work with us, then they would have to implement safety standards and greatly improve conditions. If the managers weren't willing to do that, we took our business elsewhere. It was – and still is – extremely gratifying to see the improvements we were able to instigate and to know we were improving the lives of the factory workers and their families.

Prime: *You don't have to invest in China. What are the risks there for you and others and how have those risks changed over time?*

Ellyson: I wasn't completely aware of all the risks of doing business in China when I first began working there, but I thought I could figure it out as I went along. In general, the main areas of risk include environmental risks like floods and earthquakes and political disruptions that can shut down businesses and halt transportation. East West Manufacturing deals with quality risks where we have to educate and supervise the Chinese workers to ensure each and every shipment meets our clients' quality standards. We clearly communicate and document quality expectations in advance and work closely with the factory managers throughout the manufacturing process.

The key to mitigating all of these risks is diversifying the process. For example, both environmental and governmental upheavals can disrupt a supply chain, so we have to develop multiple sources of materials and manufacturing sites. That way, manufacturing can continue without a disastrous interruption, and you can also move products around to take maximum advantage of savings – either raw material or labor costs. And by diversifying, I mean diversifying within and beyond China. There are many more options both in China and other developing countries than there used to be, offering customers security, flexibility and maximum competitiveness.

Prime: *How has East West Manufacturing responded to the risks and to the changing opportunities?*

Ellyson: We strategically match products to expertise, helping our clients take advantage of local production skills and strengths. We pre-qualify our suppliers on critical manufacturing capabilities, competitiveness, IP stewardship, safety and labor practices. And, most importantly, we believe in having "feet on the street." In other words, we maintain a significant presence in each country of manufacture, whether working with sub-suppliers or a fully owned factory, to understand the local culture, negotiate the best pricing and manage suppliers' performance.

When we manufacture over $1 million worth of products for a customer, we automatically add multiple suppliers. As I mentioned above, we have diversified both raw materials sourcing and manufacturing facilities outside of China to India and Vietnam, because I feel certain Chinese labor costs will continue to rise, and there is always a risk of political change. This year, we are working towards being able to sell products inside China, rather than shipping everything overseas, to take advantage of this emerging market. Some of our competitors are moving further west into China, but I believe it makes more sense to diversity outside of China.

Prime: One of the biggest challenges in your business must be quality control. How do you manage this? Does your strategy on quality control differ in China as compared with other countries?

Ellyson: No matter what country we are working in, it all starts by understanding what our customers' quality requirements are and documenting those requirements in advance. From there, we work closely with the factory manager every step of the way, testing and inspecting raw materials as well as each shipment of finished product. I tell people it's like baking a cake. The customer tells us what the cake must look, smell and taste like. We procure quality ingredients for the recipe. The factory bakes the cake. Our oversight ensures the ingredients are acceptable, the recipe is being followed and the end product – the cake – is exactly as requested. Quality assurance is built into every step of the process.

Prime: What is your favorite story from your China experiences?

Ellyson: There are so many, it's hard to choose, but I am especially proud of how we established our office in Shenzhen, China. In the beginning, we wanted to find a Chinese engineer with the education and experience to run our Shenzhen operation. Despite an intensive search, we couldn't find someone with our original requirements, but we found Kenny, who had the education and talent, but not the experience. We decided to take a chance with him, but as Plan B, we hired Matt, an engineer from Texas who had been living in China, studying Mandarin, and was now working for a U.K.-based manufacturer. We thought Matt could step in if Kenny didn't work out.

Kenny more than "worked out." He exceeded our expectations and has become a valued member of East West Manufacturing's senior staff, and a key reason for our Shenzhen operation's success. Matt turned out to be the perfect person to oversee our new factory in Vietnam, and thanks to him, we were able to get new facility operational very quickly. Both men have made tremendous contributions to our company's growth.

Prime: Being in an outsourcing business, you probably are often asked why you are not manufacturing more in the U.S. What is your response?

Ellyson: We call what we do for our customers "Domestic Offshore Manufacturing." In a nutshell, we oversee the planning, design and implementation of offshore product manufacturing for Western-based original equipment manufacturers and distributors. We marry the quality control typically found in domestic manufacturing with the cost- savings of offshore manufacturing. The model makes sense for a number of U.S.-based businesses seeking to stay competitive in their markets. It doesn't mean we take all of their manufacturing offshore. We take some of the component manufacturing offshore so our customers can reap the benefits of the expertise available in other countries and realize cost savings. It's not black-and-white or all-or-nothing in manufacturing, meaning many products are manufactured in one or more locations and assembled elsewhere. Take cars for example. Even the ones touted as "American made" have components manufactured all over the world. The final assembly takes place in the U.S. The same is true with computers. China is where most circuit boards are now manufactured and then shipped overseas for final assembly. Maybe down the road, East West Manufacturing will set up our own manufacturing facility in the U.S. for final assembly. In the meantime, because of what we do, our customers are able to competitively price their products and grow their market share.

Prime: *What should policy makers in the U.S. do to improve the domestic environment for manufacturing and for business more generally?*

Ellyson: In my opinion, we've completely lost our way in terms of attracting manufacturing to the U.S. Taxes are the biggest culprit. The United States levies the highest corporate taxes in the world and fails to incentivize investment at the federal level. Compare that to any other industrial country trying to attract manufacturing. For example, if I go to Vietnam and China, I pay zero tax for the first five years and half the corporate rate for the next five years. Here at home, I pay almost 40 percent in taxes from day one. When you start a business, those early years are crucial and taxes take a huge percent. How can we expect people to begin businesses when the tax burden is so high? We could overcome the high labor costs in the U.S. if we could reduce taxes and regulations. The other thing that has to happen is healthcare reform. Healthcare costs severely impact businesses. In our own company, our healthcare costs just increased 20 percent this past year, which is a big deal for our bottom line. Everyone talks about labor costs in the U.S., but the reality is that healthcare costs are going up more than labor costs.

As for innovation, we must improve our regulatory and government agencies like the U.S. Patent Office. In China, the average lead time to obtain a patent is two-to-three years. In the U.S. the average lead time is eight-to-nine years. That sort of bureaucratic red tape discourages innovation, rather than supporting and encouraging it. One of our engineers may come up with a great idea to improve efficiency, but if I know it will take up to nine years before we have intellectual property protection via patent approval, I am not going to move forward with the idea.

Prime: *Do you think it is likely the U.S. will take these steps?*

Ellyson: Not anytime soon. Sadly, I believe things have to get even worse before we take the necessary actions to make them better. I don't think these are political issues, I think they're incompetence issues. It's as if our political leaders are only looking at short-term ideas to solve long-term problems. For example, the new jobs bill recently proposed by the president is full of immediate, short-term recommendations. Those of us running a business have to think long-term, and I don't see that happening in our government.

Another problem is the divisiveness of our elected officials. I don't remember ever having such a polarized Congress. I think the citizens of this country are tired of all the bickering and want our elected leaders to work together to solve the serious economic issues the U.S. is facing. At the same time, we seem to be blind to our competition. We're not taking note of what other countries are doing to obtain and maintain a competitive advantage. Instead, we're distracted by wars, debt, joblessness and immigration issues and are taking our focus away from business productivity.

Prime: *I have heard you argue that the U.S. needs to maintain some manufacturing in order to ensure innovation. What is the connection and why is this so important?*

Ellyson: If you disconnect yourself entirely from manufacturing, you become removed from the processes that stimulate innovation. Ideas for how to make things better, faster and cheaper come from people who work day-to-day in manufacturing.

Prime: *Although manufacturing's share of employment has fallen substantially, the U.S. still has a large manufacturing base in terms of value. Is a large value base—if we maintain it—sufficient to support innovation from your perspective?*

Ellyson: No, it is not. We need to become more creative to attract more manufacturing here. Every manufacturing job creates service sector jobs like dry cleaning, grocery stores, and so forth. The reality is we are in a competitive global market. China is going after our high-tech industry, for example. It's not enough to hang onto the research and development functions. Look at Apple. They have around 50,000 employees designing their products, but they sub out the manufacturing of those products to another company with a million employees. That tells me it takes a million people to make what 50,000 people design. So, you can't create enough jobs with just R&D. You have to hang on to the manufacturing, too.

Prime: *Do you see Chinese companies as primarily competitors, or as coopera-tive partners in a global production networks that help create value for everyone?*

Ellyson: They're both and we're shifting from one to another. We're moving from a cooperative base that supports many multi-national companies to a competi-tive environment. Chinese companies created their foundation by serving as our suppliers, but now they're going to be aggressively looking for brands to own that will compete against our brands. The Chinese want the same success we've had and they understand you're not going to get there by making prod-ucts for other companies.

Prime: *Any final thoughts?*

Ellyson: You often hear that China is unfairly manipulating its currency. In some respects this is true, but at the moment I don't think it is undervalued. Most people don't realize that just a few years ago, China's currency was trading at 8.78 Yuan to the U.S. dollar and now it's at 6.38. That's a shift of nearly 30%. Even if the currency moves another 15-20 percent to the dollar, it's not going to have a major impact on our trade imbalance. If anything a higher currency will just push more manufacturing to other lower-cost countries.

It's true that China exports more products to the U.S. than it imports from us, but the reverse is true for China and the rest of the world. In total, China consumes more than it exports. Nevertheless, a lot of people are calling for tax-ing products coming into this country from China. Well, guess what? China is not the cheapest country for manufacturing any more and if we start taxing them, do you really think companies will move their production back to the U.S.? No – they'll go to Vietnam, Indonesia, India or another low cost coun-try. The only thing taxing products from China will help is in creating a trade war, which we definitely don't need right now.

China is evolving and we've got to find ways to work together. Here at home, we should be focusing on high tech products (like bio and energy) that aren't as sensitive to labor costs and incentivize manufacturing so we can compete in the new global reality. We must implement long-term programs like permanent R&D tax credits, lower corporate taxes, elimination of capital gains and Sarbanes-Oxley, reduced healthcare costs, faster patent processes and stopping the "brain drain" to other countries.

Let's not view China as a threat. Instead, let's look at China as a partner with whom we can make positive changes.

Manned Space Program and Making of Chinese National Identity

Liang Yao
Vol.10, No.1
2011

With the successful launch of the Shenzhou V on October 15, 2003, China became the third country in the world that could independently send people into space. The accomplishment enkindled a worldwide debate around China's success. Many western scholars believe that China's manned spaceflight program aims to promote its economic, military, scientific and technological capability. They see the space program-a dual-use technology that either has a civil use or military applications-as one of the most important military strategies of the CCP, which could reinforce communist China's military strength, as well as build and guarantee its geopolitical and strategic influences. In May 1999, The Cox Report generated by a U.S. Congressional committee claimed that for the CCP, the ultimate goal of promoting civilian economy is to support the building of modern military weapons for the PLA. It is estimated that China's current missile range involves a wide area that directly threatens the United States' national security. The Cox Report also asserts the Chinese scientist Qian Xuesen, founding father of the Chinese space program, was a spy who stole American missile technologies to boost the development of Chinese ballistic missiles.[1] Although there are many exaggerations in the Cox Report, it reveals great uneasiness of the western world. Admittedly there might be military consideration as well as other incentives such as economy, science and technology; however, on the other hand, the manned space program reflects the building of Chinese national identity. Based on Chinese government reports and newspapers, this article demonstrates that China's

---

1   Cox report, *http://www.house.gov/coxreport/, accesses by 2010-3-6*

human spaceflight was not merely a product of China's economic, military, science and technology development concerns which have been already fully discussed by many scholars, rather it was a product of the national identity-making and a demand of the national spirit.

China's space program was initiated early in 1956 when Qian Xuesen (Tsien Hsue-shen), one of China's most senior scientists, urged China's leaders to consider the possibilities of interplanetary space flight, even as China was confronting one of the worst famines in Chinese history.[2] In the 1970s, Qian brought forward a manned spaceflight proposal called the "714" project. However because of the weakness of the national power, backwardness of research ability and experience, lack of funding, and domestic political crises, the project was put aside by Chairman Mao. The 1970s was an era when the Chinese pulled together to reconstruct their newborn country with confidence and enthusiasm. It also was an era full of political movements that distracted the PRC's development agenda. When Mao's heir apparent, Minister of Defense Linbiao, was killed in an air crash in Mongolia on September, 13, 1971, Mao accused Linbiao and his group of planning a coup. Because of the bad economy resulting from the war and severe famine in the '60s, it was too hard for the Chinese government to support a project as costly as the space program. Mao emphasized the nation must take care of terrestrial needs first; space could come later. The space program was still laid aside when Deng Xiaoping took office. It was not resumed until January 1992. Unlike in the '70s, the Chinese government seemed quite ambitious and determined in the '90s. They demanded the program have a great technological breakthrough before 1998, and make every effort to launch an airship in 1999.[3] Why did China push its manned spaceflight program so hard in the '90s when it showed such reluctance during the '70s?

First of all, many social crises went around in the last decade of the 20th century that threatened China's national solidarity and prestige. Deng Xiaoping's reform and open policy in 1978 turned China from a plan-oriented economy to a market-oriented economy, a new road to modernization. However, according to Yongnian Zheng, unlike many other countries whose modernization and centralization were almost identical, in modern China, modernization was characterized by decentralization. Decentralization promoted rapid economic growth and dramatic social changes on the one hand, but led to a nationwide crisis on the other such as the deterioration of national identity, traditional values, Marxist beliefs

2   By Peter J Brown, "China's space pioneer under the microscope", Copyright 2009 Asia Times Online (Holdings) Ltd, http://www.atimes.com/atimes/China/KH27Ad01.html, accessed by 2010-3-8

3   Xinhua News, Sep.24, 2008. "China's manned spaceflight program", http://www.cnsa.gov.cn/n615708/n2243881/n2243887/166780.html, accessed by 2010-1-10.

and Maoist faith.[4] The rise of separatists in Tibet and Xinjiang in the post-Mao period, the Tiananmen Square protests of 1989[5] and the collapse of the Soviet Union caused the Chinese government to rouse national confidence and prestige, and redefine China's national identity in the new condition home and abroad.

Secondly, a trend of technocracy emerged in contemporary China. Technological determinism became a dominant ideology with Chinese politicians. Science and technology appeared to be the panacea to all social problems. Michael Adas points out that after the Industrial Revolution, science and technology replaced religion as the dominant ideology in western societies.[6] So it was in modern China. Influenced by a "hundred years of humiliation" since the Opium War, Chinese people deeply believed their backwardness in science and technology left them vulnerable to attack. As early as late Qing Dynasty, Chinese intellectuals began to notice the important role of science and technology in the takeoff of western countries. To save the crumbling Qing Dynasty, they initiated a Self-Strengthening movement called tiyong (Chinese fundamentals and western technology). In 1919, science again was used as one of the slogans in China's New Culture Movement aimed at awakening and saving China from the imperialist aggressions. In the PRC, by adopting and interpreting Marxist theory as one of the CCP's theoretical guides, the Chinese people again were convinced by technological determinism. Marx's classical saying: "The hand-mill gives you society with the feudal lord; the steam-mill, society with the industrial capitalist"[7] indicates the level of technology represents the degree of development of a society. Accordingly, Deng Xiaoping raised a slogan in the 1980s that "science and technology are the primary productive force," encouraging Chinese to use science, technology and education to revive the greatness of the nation. Since then, numbers of science and engineering majors in Chinese universities are expanding greatly and quickly, compared to liberal arts majors. Scientists and engineers soon became heroes in Chinese people's minds. More and more Chinese children dreamed of being scientists and engineers when they grew up; more and more students chose science and engineering majors; even more notably, more and more officers in Chinese government had science or engineering education backgrounds since the 1980s. In a study on the 16th Central Committee of the CCP, Li Cheng and Lynn White

---

4   Yongnian Zheng, *Discovering Chinese Nationalism in China, Modernization, Identity, and International Relations, Cambridge University Press, 1999. P.21.*

5   *The Tiananmen Square protests of 1989, referred to in most of the world as the Tiananmen Square massacre, were a series of demonstrations in and near Tiananmen Square in Beijing in the PRC beginning on 14 April 1989. Led mainly by students and intellectuals, the protest's aims were pro-democracy and anti-corruption. The movement lasted seven weeks, ended with a crackdown by the PRC government.*

6   Michael Adas, *Machines as the Measure of Men: Science, Technology and Ideologies of Western Dominance, Ithaca : Cornell University Press, 1989.*

7   Karl Marx, *The Poverty of Philosophy, Progress Publishers, 1955. Chapter 2, part I.*

concluded that throughout the history of the PRC, "social scientists have usually been marginalized and occasionally despised."[8] They noted that among the full members of the 15th (1997) and 16th (2002) CCs who have college degrees, 55.6% had engineering and science majors in the 15th CC, and 45.5% in the 16th CC.[9] Cheng and White as well as other scholars assumed that post-Mao China has a trend of technocracy in which technocrats emerged as the core leadership in the CCP. Many Chinese politicians, especially those who have engineering degrees, believe science and technology are the most effective way to solve all the problems in China.

Facing crises home and abroad on the one hand, having technological determinism ideology and the trend of technocracy on the other, it is not surprising to see post-Mao China using concrete technology to rebuild its endangered national identity. In order to highlight "Chineseness" and "Greatness," the Chinese government constructed a series of concrete images to identify the Chinese nation and its long progressive history. This intention could be seen apparently in all propaganda at home and abroad, especially at the opening celebration of 2008 Olympics in Beijing, in which China's Four Great Inventions - paper making, printing, the compass and gunpowder - were well displayed. It provided an impression that China's civilization is continuous and progressive, represented by a series of advanced scientific and technological achievements. In the Qin Dynasty (770 BC), China built one of the Seven Wonders in the world, The Great Wall; The Four Great Inventions represented the great achievements from the Han to Song Dynasties; Zheng He's voyage to the Indian Ocean in the Ming Dynasty revealed that Chinese navigation technology was at the top of the world at that time. For the CCP, the culture of ancient China was the root of the Chinese nation, and these images representing Chinese civilization were always sources of pride for the Chinese. When it comes to communist China, the CCP again strived to use concrete images to continue its national image-making. Even in the 1950s and '60s, when the Mao administration was so welcomed, trusted, and esteemed by the mass, they still drastically extolled their satellites and atomic bomb, showing how great the nation was and how wise the leadership of the CCP.

However, with the domestic policy change since the '80s, tensions grew gradually. The new generation of the CCP leadership, most of whom were technocrats, felt a lack of image consistency. How to mitigate pressure at home and abroad, how to keep authority, how to continuously inspire people's national pride, and how to keep the consistency of the national image became important issues for the CCP in the post-Mao era. The manned spaceflight program was well fit for

---

8   Li Cheng and Lynn White, "The Sixteenth Central Committee of The Chinese Communist Party", *Asian Survey*, July 2003, P553-97.
9   Ibid.

these considerations.

As expected, soon after the success of the Shenzhou V, immense enthusiasm swept the country. This inspiring news dominated the headlines of China's main newspapers, magazines and TV news right after the successful flight. People's Daily ran 100,000 extra copies which were quickly snapped up, as did other papers. Schoolchildren drew pictures of spaceflights and showed them to press and television. In addition, 10.2 million stamps were printed in Yang Liwei's honor.[10]

Interestingly, Chinese people throughout the country did not know the news until the rocket was safely and steadily flying in space, when success was fully guaranteed by the experts. It was revealed later that journalists from all the major mass media had already congregated at the launch site with sufficient preparations at the very beginning, but they were commanded to hold the news and report live as soon as the mission was guaranteed successful. Interestingly too, Jiang Zeming, China's president at that time, had not been to the site. Instead, Hu Jingtao represented the government at the exciting moment. Obviously, it was intentionally planned by the government since manned spaceflight was not simply a technological issue for China, it also was an image project, which could not be stained by any deficiencies.

As soon as experts announced the success of the Shenzhou V, Hu Jingtao represented Jiang Zeming by giving a speech immediately from the launch site, extolling the virtues of China's manned spaceflight for the first time. He highly praised hardworking, enterprising, serious-minded, innovative, factualistic and cooperative workers and researchers in the manned spaceflight program. These characteristics were dubbed the "spaceflight virtues." In the speech, he compared the "spaceflight virtues" to the virtues shown in the making of a bomb, missile and satellite in the Mao period, and proclaimed they were the essence for the revival of the Great.[11]

After the successful launch of the Shenzhou V, the Chinese government held ceremonies for each launch and the main leaders gave celebratory speeches every time. On November 26, 2005, President Hu Jingtao gave another inspiring address for Shenzhou VI, in which he stressed the important role of science and technology in promoting economy and education. Once again he highly extolled the spaceflight virtues, which took up half of his speech. He said, "The manned spaceflight virtues are a development of the virtues of Liang Dan Yi Xing (bomb, missile and satellite) in the new era. They vividly represent patriotism, nationalism and reformism. In the road of constructing socialistic modernization, we should

10   Brian Harvey, *China's Space Program - From Conception to Manned Spaceflight*, Springer Praxis, UK, 2004. P13.
11   *Jie Fang Jun Newspaper (PLA Newspaper)*, Oct.16, 2003, http://www.mod.gov.cn/leader/2003-10/16/content_3074004.htm, accessed by 2010-1-23.

greatly publicize the spaceflight virtues over the whole society in order to increase the national pride and confidence, and intensify the national solidarity...."[12] Compared to Hu's endeavor in expatiating on the manned spaceflight virtues, the economic and scientific benefits of this program in his address seemed very broad and unclear. In the speech, he stressed the key function of science and technology in promoting economic, social and cultural development. He particularly emphasized the importance of China's independent scientific innovation, and highly lauded the Chinese manned spaceflight as a representation of "Made in China project" in order to encourage more independent innovations. Two themes were apparent in Hu's speech, the manned spaceflight virtues and "Chineseness." As a result, a neutral technology was tinted by certain identity that was not neutral any more. The manned spaceflight first of all was marked by a nationality-Chinese. Then it became the embodiment of certain virtues-hardworking, innovative, cooperation, united, enterprising, serious-minded and factualistic etc. Combining the two, Chinese leaders endowed the concrete space technology with a new meaning, an embodiment of the national identity which is flawless, inspiring and honorable.

The Chinese government intentionally created a perfect hero image - the first Chinese astronaut, Yang Liwei - so impeccable and consummate, and encompassing all the best virtues of the Chinese nation. Without exception, all Chinese media described Yang Liwei as a good child, good student and excellent pilot inborn. According to official biographies, Yang had a "happy and tranquil childhood" and was "very intelligent and a good team leader of his playmates." Excelling in mathematics and math competitions, Yang scored high on entrance exams and went to the best middle school in his county. Joining the People's Liberation Army at the age of 18, Yang was recruited by one of the Chinese Air Force's top aviation colleges, where he earned the highest grade in every class he took. Upon graduation, he became a fighter pilot and was rated as an "elite" member of his Air Force division.[13] Yang's predisposition to be a pilot stemmed from both an excellent physical condition and a perfect psychological quality. He was a quick learner and fast reactor, neither smoking nor drinking and had solid flying knowledge and experience.[14] All in all, Yang was exactly "the right man" to take the mission.

Yang was not only technically a highly qualified pilot, he also was hardworking, friendly and humble, which were noble virtues in Chinese value. One of his colleagues commented Yang was so modest that he never talked about himself. He never mentioned his hobbies such as travel and music, and even did not express

12 *China Manned Space Engineering, Nov. 26, 2005, http://www.cmse.gov.cn/project/show. php?itemid=138. accessed by 2009-12-10*
13 *Steven J Dick and Roger D. Launius ed., Social Impact of Spaceflight, NASA, 2007. P106*
14 *China Youth, Oct.25, 2003, http://news.sina.com.cn/c/2003-10-25/04181993879.shtml. accessed by 2009-12-11*

his own individual mood. By contrast, he always regarded himself as one plain pilot in China's manned spaceflight team. In his mind, there was no individual "I," but only a collective "we."[15]

In Confucian China, one's evaluation is tightly related to one's private life. Being considerate to family is estimated as one of the most important and indispensable virtues for a gentleman. Yang also fits this model. Yang's wife, Zhang Yumei told journalists that "Yang is a considerate husband. He loved me and our family, he tried every effort to take care of the family in despite of his busy work. When I gave birth to little Ningkang (their son), Yang cooked for me every day. Although Liwei was very busy after he joined the manned spaceflight program and seldom came home, he often called home, and made every effort to accompany Ningkang and me as soon as he had some time."[16] When Yang was in space, Chinese media broadcasted nationwide that Yang called his wife and son, telling them he was fine and asking them not to worry about him.

As soon as he successfully completed China's first manned spaceflight mission, Yang Liwei was honored as one of the "top ten outstanding Youths in China," "China's spaceflight hero" (Nov. 7, 2003)[17] and awarded as "major general."[18] His news appeared on the front page of every main Chinese newspaper and dominated most of China's mass media for several days. He became a public figure overnight. After returning, he was much busier than before. Besides regular training, Yang was invited to give speeches to university students, government officers and factory workers, and was interviewed by hundreds of journalists, in which he was highly lauded.

Right after the success, members of the manned spaceflight team formed a reporting team that traveled all over the country to advocate the manned spaceflight virtues. This team was made up of Yang Liwei, manned spaceflight scientists, researchers, engineers and workers. In the year after the successful launch, this reporting team visited most of the major cities in China including Beijing, Shanghai, Tianjin, Chongqing, Shengyang, Hongkong and Macao etc., covering nearly every corner of Chinese territory. It was reported that people in all these cities welcomed the team with tremendous enthusiasm and admiration. In Tianjin, five-thousand people gathered at the exit of Jing-Jin highway, beating drums and gongs, singing and dancing to welcome the coming of the manned spaceflight team. In Chongqing, the city turned into a sea of people and flowers

---

15 *Lifeweek, Dec.9, 2003, http://www.lifeweek.com.cn/2004-01-02/000017593.shtml. access by 2009-12-11*

16 *Southern Daily, Aug.9, 2004, http://www.southcn.com/news/gdnews/sz/whz/ jj/200408090147.htm. accessed by 2009-12-11*

17 *Xin Hua News, Nov. 7, 2003, http://news.xinhuanet.com/newscenter/2003-11/07/content_1167141.htm, accessed by 2010-2-6*

18 *Xin Hua News, Jun 22, 2008, http://news.xinhuanet.com/mil/2008-07/22/content_8745772.htm, accessed by 2010-2-6*

when the visiting team passed by. In Yang Liwei's hometown Shenyang, jubilation permeated the whole city. Four-thousand people stood along the 16-mile road to welcome their hero back.[19] It was reported that during a 100-minute report in Chongqing, the audience interrupted 67 times with thunderous applause. One undergraduate student said even the most famous speechmaker would hardly receive such a welcome.[20] One third grade student in Tianjin No.7 middle school named Guo Fangjie told journalists, "Yang Liwei is a 'star' in my heart. He is also a 'star' in people's hearts in all of our country."[21]

The fervor of success was immersed in every social activity. In Haikou, the first international sand sculpture exhibition included a series of sculptures with the theme "the heaven and the earth." One was a sand statue of Yang Liwei standing on the top of the returning capsule of Shenzhou V. The 8.5-meter-high sculpture included a large Earth model at the base, and was called the highest work in the exhibition. Universities such as Tsinghua and Nankai also invited Yang Liwei to give reports to enthusiastic students. In addition, universities and high schools also held a series of activities such as scientific and technological competitions called "manned spaceflight virtues" to commit to memory the country's exciting moment and encourage the youth to learn the manned spaceflight virtues.

In short, Shenzhou V serves as one part of a series of continuous and systematic efforts by the CCP in the new era to make Chinese national images and identity at home and abroad. The CCP assigned distinctive cutting-edge technologies to each stage of Chinese history in order to show the greatness of the Chinese nation. It was far beyond party politics. Through highlighting two themes: "Science and Technology" and "Chineseness," Shenzhou V combined the great nation's ancient dream of flying into the heavens with the contemporary requirement for consolidating unity and revival, to become a new symbol in Chinese history.

References:
Books and Papers:
Adas, Michael, *Machines as the Measure of Men: Science, Technology and Ideologies of Western Dominance, Ithaca : Cornell University Press, 1989.*
Brown, Peter J, "China's space pioneer under the microscope," Copyright 2009 Asia Times Online (Holdings) Ltd, http://www.atimes.com/atimes/China/KH27Ad01.html, accessed by 2010-3-8
Dick, Steven J and Roger D. Launius ed., Social Impact of Spaceflight, NASA, 2007. P106
Harvey, Brian, China's Space Program-From Conception to Manned Spaceflight, Springer Praxis, UK, 2004. P13.
Li Cheng and Lynn White, "The Sixteenth Central Committee of The Chinese Communist Party," Asian Survey, July 2003, P553-97.
Marx, Karl The Poverty of Philosophy, Progress Publishers, 1955. Chapter 2, part I.

---

19 *People, Nov 23, 2003, http://www.people.com.cn/GB/keji/1059/2205486.html, accessed by 2010-2-7*

20 *People, Nov 23, 2003, http://www.people.com.cn/GB/keji/1059/2205486.html, accessed by 2010-2-7*

21 *Ibid.*

Zheng, Yongnian, *Discovering Chinese Nationalism in China, Modernization, Identity, and International Relations*, Cambridge University Press, 1999. P.21.

On-line Sources:

China Manned Space Engineering, Nov. 26, 2005, http://www.cmse.gov.cn/project/show.php?itemid=138. accessed by 2009-12-10.

China Youth, Oct.25, 2003, http://news.sina.com.cn/c/2003-10-25/04181993879.shtml. accessed by 2009-12-11

Jie Fang Jun Newspaper (PLA Newspaper), Oct.16, 2003, http://www.mod.gov.cn/leader/2003-10/16/content_3074004.htm, accessed by 2010-1-23.

Lifeweek, Dec. 9, 2003, http://www.lifeweek.com.cn/2004-01-02/000017593.shtml. access by 2009-12-11

People, Nov. 23, 2003, http://www.people.com.cn/GB/keji/1059/2205486.html, accessed by 2010-2-7

Southern Daily, Aug. 9, 2004, http://www.southcn.com/news/gdnews/sz/whz/jj/200408090147.htm. accessed by 2009-12-11

Xin Hua News, June 22, 2008, http://news.xinhuanet.com/mil/2008-07/22/content_8745772.htm, accessed by 2010-2-6

Xin Hua News, Nov. 7, 2003, http://news.xinhuanet.com/newscenter/2003-11/07/content_1167141.htm, accessed by 2010-2-6

Xinhua News, Nov. 11, 2003, http://news.xinhuanet.com/newscenter/2003-11/11/content_1172495.htm. accessed by 2009-12-11

Xinhua News, Sep. 24, 2008. "China's manned spaceflight program", http://www.cnsa.gov.cn/n615708/n2243881/n2243887/166780.html, accessed by 2010-1-10.

Liang Yao is a Ph.D. candidate in History, Technology and Society at the Georgia Institute of Technology, Atlanta, GA.

China and a U.S.-Iran War

John Garver
Vol. 11, No. 1
2012

Negotiations about Iran's nuclear program moved to a crucial stage in May and June of 2012. Unless Tehran accedes to international demands that it open to international inspections that verify that Iran's nuclear programs are not designed to produce nuclear weapons, a pre-emptive military strike — perhaps by Israel alone, perhaps with U.S. participation — could well result. In the midst of this escalating tension, prominent voices in the United States are urging that China could play an important role in resolving the Iran nuclear issue and averting a potential clash between Iran and the US. and/or Israel.

I believe these hopes for China are misplaced. Although there are people in China's Ministry of Foreign Affairs who believe that such a Chinese effort resulting in an accommodation between the Iran and the U.S.-led international community would serve China's interests, other voices take a far more jaundiced view of how China should deal with the United States. These bitter and hawkish views are strong in China's military. It is unlikely that any Chinese leader would want to offend the hawks, because intense maneuvering for succession to paramount power on the Politburo Standing Committee is under way in the lead-up to this fall's 18th Congress of the Chinese Communist Party (CCP) China is unlikely to use its influence to avert a U.S.-Iran clash. If it comes to war between the United States and the Islamic Republic of Iran, Beijing will do little materially to assist Iran. But neither will Beijing help the U.S. prevent, or extricate itself from, another Middle Eastern quagmire.

Dreams of China as a U.S. Partner

Some prominent voices in the U.S. hope China will use its substantial influence with Tehran to persuade it to come to a negotiated, compromise settlement with Washington. A recent monograph by three Fellows (all U.S. military officers) in the National Security Program of Harvard University's Kennedy School of Government, titled "Reaching a Negotiated Settlement on the Iranian Nuclear Program," advocates a three-pronged push for a negotiated settlement with Iran. The second prong is an approach to Tehran through China. "After failing to act decisively to stop the bloodshed in Syria," said the report "China now has an opportunity to demonstrate global leadership to reach an acceptable agreement and prevent a military conflict from affecting energy supplies coming from the Middle East."[1]

The authors of the Harvard monograph elaborate the multiple ways in which Chinese mediation would serve China's own interests. War would be averted that might otherwise disrupt China's oil imports, make those oil imports expensive and depress foreign markets for China's exports. Chinese mediation would demonstrate that its growing influence would be used responsibly to uphold peace. China would win Washington's gratitude for working in tandem with U.S. diplomacy rather than as a peer competitor. Beijing also would win the gratitude of Iran for helping it avert war, further demonstrating to Iran the utility of friendship with China. The Harvard paper also documents via Wikileaks memoranda that China's Ministry of Foreign Affairs served as an intermediary between Washington and Tehran in the first year of the Obama Administration, when the new team in Washington was pushing to reset U.S. ties with both Tehran and Beijing.

These arguments are all solid. Some of them are sourced to this author's own writings. But ultimately, Beijing is not likely to use its influence to help the United States avoid or extricate itself from war or chronic militarized confrontation with the Islamic Republic of Iran. Weighted against the interests enumerated above, is the global strategic reality that China benefits from having the United States bogged down in chronic conflict with Iran in the Persian Gulf.

Another recent article by two analysts in well-connected think tanks and published in the journal Foreign Policy argues that U.S. movement toward a strike against Iran would "persuade Beijing and Tehran alike that this option [of U.S. attack] is the alternative to full compliance with international sanctions." It says further, "Establishing a credible military threat to Iran" and a "credible U.S. threat to disarm the Iranian regime," would compel China's leaders to drop their sup-

---

1   LTC John Digiambattista, LTC David Horan, LTC Matthew R. Lewis, CDR John Spencer, *Reaching a Negotiated Settlement on the Iranian Nuclear Program, John F. Kennedy School of Government, National Security Program, 2012. The other two prongs were 1) U.S. lowering its demands from complete suspension of nuclear enrichment to a limited and fully transparent enrichment program, and 2) U.S. and Israeli preparations for a military strike to make credible the threat of use of force.*

port for Iran.[2] Since a U.S.-Iran war would imperil China's oil supplies from the Gulf, so the argument goes, confronting Beijing with that possibility would force Beijing to use its influence with Tehran to submit to U.S. terms. Again these estimates of China's calculations seem misplaced. They fly in the face of China's perception of a vast U.S. conspiracy against China and of what is required to foil U.S. hostile strategy toward China.

Chinese Realpolitik

A recent essay by Wang Jisi lays out the zero-sum worldview increasingly dominating elite Chinese thinking about the United States.[3] Wang is dean of Beijing University's School of International Studies, advisor to the Chinese Communist Party and Ministry of Foreign Affairs and guest professor at the PLA's National Defense University. The monograph came out under the imprimatur of the Brookings Institute.

Wang Jisi paints a gloomy but dominant Chinese perspective. "It is strongly believed in China," he writes, "that the ultimate goal of the Untied States in world affairs is to maintain its hegemony and dominance and, as a result, Washington will attempt to prevent the emerging powers, in particular China, from achieving their goal and enhancing their stature." The perception that the United States "is China's greatest national security threat," Wang writes, is "especially widely shared in China's defense and security establishments and in the Communist Party's ideological organizations." Washington is using "sinister designs" involving human rights issues to "sabotage the Communist leadership and turn China into [a] vassal state." Washington has also "strengthened security ties with a number of China's neighbors" including two states [India and Vietnam] "that once fought border wars with and still have territorial disputes with China." A desire to encircle China has inspired the "pivot of U.S. strategic forces to Asia" under President Barack Obama.

U.S. policy toward Iran and the Persian Gulf is seen as a piece of the U.S. drive for global hegemony, Wang continues. U.S. Middle Eastern policy, including the war in Iraq, is seen in China as "driven by desire to control global oil supplies." Of course, if Washington does that, it will be better able to prevent China's emergence. U.S. policy toward Iran is seen in China as "driven more by an American desire to change the political structure of Iran and the geopolitical picture of the Middle East than by its declared goal of keeping the Iranians from obtain-

---

2   Michael Singh, Jacqueline Newmyer Deal, "China's Iranian Gambit," Foreign Policy, October 31, 2011. www.foreignpolicy.com Singh is managing director of the Washington Institute and former director for Middle East Affairs on the National Security Council. Deal is a Senior Fellow with the Foreign Policy Research Institute in Philadelphia

3   Kenneth Lieberthal, Wang Jisi, "Addressing U.S.-China Strategic Mistrust," John L. Thornton China Center Monograph Series, No. 4, March 2012. Brookings Institution.

ing nuclear weapons." Non-proliferation concerns, such as human rights or climate change considerations, are mere ploys serving to prop up U.S. domination. Following the 9/11 attacks, Wang reports, "China foresaw a twenty-year-long strategic opportunity in foreign affairs, during which it could focus on domestic tasks centered on economic growth." Now, however, with the Obama Administration's withdrawal from Iraq and Afghanistan, "there has arisen a stronger Chinese suspicion that the Untied States will move its strategic spearhead away from the Greater Middle East and redirect it at China as its greatest security threat."

From the perspective of this jaundiced view of U.S. policy, why would China help the United States achieve the negotiated, but internationally supervised, abstention from research and development of nuclear weapons? Such aid would constitute a step toward Iranian subordination to American domination in the Gulf. Why would China help the United States avoid another costly war in the Persian Gulf and facilitate Washington's "pivot to Asia," targeting China? Even more, an Iran-U.S. war might tie the United States down in West Asia for a number of years, draining U.S. treasure and national will, while giving China several more years to expand its economy. Another American war or confrontation in the Persian Gulf certainly would cause serious economic problems for China. But it would significantly strengthen China's national security against the United States. Would economic interests trump global strategic calculations? And what Chinese leader would want to position himself as helping the American hegemonists strengthen their anti-China containment schemes?

The near-consensus view of China's top foreign policy analysts is that the United States has seized the opportunity of the "extremely unbalanced international situation" created by the collapse of the Soviet Union to launch an aggressive drive to bring the oil of the Middle East under full U.S. control. In China's view, this is the objective behind sanctions, military deployments to the Gulf, threats of attack, actual wars and regime change in Afghanistan, Iraq, and perhaps next, Iran. Washington wants to control the oil of the Persian Gulf, the Chinese narrative continues, in order to be able to turn the spigot on or off to the consumers of that oil — India, Japan, Europe and, of course, China. Iran, a proud, ambitious, and powerful country, is now in Washington's crosshairs. It seems to be Iran's turn for U.S-style subordination via regime change — again, in China's view.

Early in the post-Soviet period, Beijing decided it would not oppose or challenge the United States in the Middle East. Precisely because that region was the focus of Washington's drive for global domination, opposition or challenge by China would be extremely dangerous. It could have undermined the Sino-American comity upon which China's extremely successful post-1978 development drive was predicated.

But fortunately for Beijing, Chinese analysts concluded that China did not need to oppose or challenge the United States in the Middle East. The United States drive for hegemony in the Gulf and in the world would be defeated by the resistance of the peoples of various countries, such as Afghanistan and Iraq, and now, perhaps, Iran.

During the 2003-2010 U.S. war in Iraq, the universal refrain in China's media was that the United States was rapidly exhausting itself in the quagmires of Iraq and Afghanistan. If the United States, in its reckless arrogance, wants to undertake yet another adventure — so be it. Let it go ahead, although again this sort of judgment cannot be rendered in public. In the event of a U.S.-Iran war, China would not, of course, endanger its vital economic relationship with the United States, but it would stand ideologically foursquare behind Tehran, would garner political capital across the non-Western world by touting its opposition to U.S. warmongering, and would find ways to assist Tehran's cause, even while continuing friendly cooperative ties with the United States in areas of common interest and agreement.

In the event of a U.S.-Iranian war, China's propaganda apparatus would stand with Iran. American warmongering would be juxtaposed against China's peaceful diplomacy and peaceful rise. China's diplomacy would be neutral but China would find ways to assist Tehran and confound Washington, though both would be done ambiguously. China's "normal economic relations" with Iran would continue, and Beijing would resist U.S. efforts to narrow those economic ties. China would probably not supply arms to Iran; that work already has been done. But Chinese military observers would probably watch closely how well China-supplied weapons worked in the field against U.S. forces.

To imagine that China would help the U.S. avert another Middle East quagmire is a serious misreading of China's views and policies. It is an egregious example of script-writing in which one predicts how others will act on the basis of one's own perceptions and objectives. In the hardheaded realist atmosphere of foreign policy decision-making circles in Beijing, a U.S.-Iranian war would not be antithetical to Chinese interests — although this could never be said openly. Chinese analysts currently view Washington as attempting to extricate itself from Iraq and Afghanistan in order to shift forces and focus to East Asia, to better contain China. If Washington undertakes a new and probably bigger Middle Eastern war, China's global strategic situation would not be diminished. And who knows, perhaps the Americans will finally exhaust themselves and become much more willing to accommodate China's rise.

John Garver, Ph.D. is professor of international relations at the Sam Nunn School of International Affairs, Georgia Institute of Technology, Atlanta, Georgia.

China's Growing Presence in Latin America: Implications for U.S. and Chinese Presence in the Region

Michael Cerna
Vol. 10, No. 1
2011

Introduction

A major talking point in the U.S. media today is the alleged weakening of American influence in the world. The common perception is that power is shifting to East Asia, and particularly to China, with ramifications globally and especially close to home in Latin America. China's economic emergence over the last decade has sent shockwaves through the region, causing economic policy shifts and realignment of markets toward the reawakened dragon. While the U.S. has a strong history of moving to block outside political influence in Latin America, its attention of late has been focused on Iraq and Afghanistan, and the region has gradually fallen lower and lower on America's list of priorities. China has been all too willing to fill any void. However, the numbers show that, despite the rapid growth of the Chinese economy, the U.S. remains the central figure in economic relations with Latin America by an enormous margin. Yet, there are trends that should at least concern the United States. Exactly how worried should the U.S. be about China's growing influence in Latin America? Is China on its way to overtaking the U.S. as the region's primary trade partner? Are China's motivations strictly economic or is there an underlying political driver behind China's actions that should warrant concern from the U.S.? Perhaps most important, is trade with Latin America a zero-sum game, or is it possible for both China and the United States to benefit from Latin America's growth? These are the questions that this article will attempt to answer.

Historical Roots

In March 2011, U.S. President Barack Obama met with leaders and officials in Brazil, Chile and El Salvador. Mr. Obama made this visit amid growing Chinese power in the region. The trip marked the first time President Obama had visited Latin America since becoming President. By comparison, at this point in Hu Jintao's presidency, the Chinese president already had visited four countries, including Brazil, where he signed 39 bilateral agreements and announced $100 billion in investments. While Mr. Obama was well-received during his trip, the most common response in those countries was that the trip was symbolic but not very substantive. Obama's visit did not reflect any shift in policy. Many of the major statements these countries hoped for (such as a call for Brazil's permanent place on the U.N. Security Council), in fact, were not made. Mr. Obama admitted on his trip: "There have been times when the United States took this region for granted," according to the Latin American Herald Tribune. Those times are not yet in the distant past and there are fears this administration is making mistakes similar to ones in the past. After promising during his 2000 election campaign to correct Washington's indifference to Latin America, George W. Bush was accused of turning his back on the region in favor of more pressing issues in the wake of the September 11 attacks. The President showed no concern for a growing Chinese influence in the hemisphere, and China put both feet inside before anyone in Washington seemed to realize the door was open. This was a move China had planned during the administration of George H.W. Bush.

In 1990, only a year after China gunned down protesters in the Tiananmen Square demonstrations, President Yang Shangkun visited five countries in Latin America. His trip was the first of an increasing number of high-level missions that laid the foundation for what he described as "a new international political and economic order" (McCarthy, 2008). However, the depth to which China would be involved with the region did not expose itself for almost a decade. In 2001, then-Chinese President Jiang Zemin completed a 12-day mission to cement economic ties with Latin America. Key countries on his itinerary included Brazil Argentina, and Venezuela. Li Peng, Chairman of the Standing Committee of the People's National Congress, followed up with more visits in November 2001. Then in November 2004, in what may one day be considered the turning point of Latin America's shift away from U.S. relations, President Hu Jintao flew to Argentina, Brazil, Chile and Cuba, where he announced the aforementioned $100 billion in investments over the next 10 years (Painter, 2008). His goal was that by 2010 the amount of two-way trade between with the region would equal $100 billion. Yet not even China could have expected such incredible results.

By 2007 two-way trade between China and Latin America had already eclipsed $100 billion, almost 50% more than the previous year and three years ahead of schedule. In 2008, two-way trade and investment reached $140 billion, with approximately $120 billion devoted to bilateral trade (Miller, 2009). China appears to be slowly closing the gap on the U.S. In 2009, Latin American exports to China jumped nine times, reaching $41.3 billion, almost 7% of all Latin American exports, according to Kevin Gallagher of The Guardian. U.S. exports and imports with the entire region are still vastly greater than China's, but year by year, China is catching up and in some countries, surpassing the U.S.

Even though China has become a major player over the past decade, trade between the China and Latin America still pales in comparison to Latin American-U.S. trade. Regional trade with the U.S. totals $560 billion compared to just over $140 billion in trade with China. But the trend is significant when looking at where China was in 2000 ($13 billion) (Painter, 2008). When we look at Latin American trade over the past decade with both the U.S. and China, one would find that the percentage of trade is slightly shifting. At the beginning of the 2000s the U.S. had more than half of the trade with the region; China had less than 10% for China. Now the U.S. has roughly the same amount of total trade, but China is now nearing 12%. Going back a little further, total U.S. trade in Latin America increased from 7.2% in 1996 to 8.3% in 2009 (Hornbeck, 2011). However, Mexico is the largest trading partner of the U.S., which brings that number up significantly. If trade with Mexico through NAFTA is taken away, U.S. trade growth with Latin America is even less impressive. Meanwhile, Sino-Latin American trade increased tenfold over the last decade and investment has also increased.

China's search for commodities

China's thirst for natural resources has sent the country in search of sustainable supplies of oil, soy and iron ore. In South America, China has found some of the most well-endowed partners in the world. China is devouring Latin American commodities and eyeing a market of 500 million people. "Countries in South America have arable land and need our technology and investment, and they welcome our companies. It's a win-win solution," said Wang Yunkun, deputy director of the Agriculture and Rural Affairs Committee of the National People's Congress, as reported by MercoPress. In 2006, more than 36% of Chile's total exports were directed toward Asia, with China taking 12% of the total. Chile was the first Latin American country to complete a major bilateral trade agreement with China (Santiso, 2007). Since then China has looked beyond Chile, also targeting Brazil, Venezuela, Ecuador, Argentina and Peru.

In 2009, China became Brazil's largest single export market, eclipsing the U.S. for the first time in history. Later, Brazil's then-president, Luiz Inacio Lula da Silva, and his Chinese counterpart, Hu Jintao, signed an agreement that allowed the China Development Bank and Sinopec to loan Brazil's state-controlled oil company, Petrobras, $10 billion in return for as many as 200,000 barrels a day of crude oil for ten years (Economist, 2009). This is but one example of how China is seizing lending opportunities in Latin America when traditional lenders such as the Inter-American Development Bank are being pushed to their limits. "Just one of China's loans, the $10 billion for Brazil's national oil company, is almost as much as the $11.2 billion in all approved financing by the Inter-American Bank in 2008," according to The New York Times.

It was not only in Brazil that China went after oil. In order to meet rising industrial needs and consumer demand, China has pursued investments and agreements with a variety of Latin American oil producers. In 2007 Venezuela agreed to a $6 billion joint investment fund for infrastructure projects at home and for oil refineries in China able to process Venezuelan heavy crude oil (Santiso, 2007). Venezuela planned to increase oil exports to China by 300,000 barrels per day. Then in 2009, Venezuela announced a $16 billion investment deal with the Chinese National Petroleum Corporation (CNPC) for oil exploration in the Orinoco River to develop heavy crude oil resources (Economist, 2009). Meanwhile, the CNPC has invested $300 million in technology to use Venezuela's Orimulsion fuel in Chinese power plants. This exemplifies Venezuela's desire to break away from the U.S. During a visit to China in 2004, President Chavez said shifting exports to China would help end dependency on sales to the United States (Johnson, 2005).

In 2003, China bid on rights to Ecuador's major oil fields. Also in 2003, the China's CNPC acquired a stake in the Argentine oil and gas firm Pluspetrol, which operates in northern Argentina and Peru. In August of 2009, the CNPC bid at least $17 million for 84% stake in YPF, Argentina's largest oil company (Economist, 2009).

China is interested in more than just oil. Deutsche Bank researcher Tamara Trinh states that as China's agricultural demands have risen sharply in the last decade, soy has been a major export to China from Argentina and Brazil. China accounts for almost 40% of the world's soybean imports and Latin America's vast agricultural sector is a perfect match for China's needs.

There is no denying that there are some positive effects for both sides that pave the way for increasing relations. Trinh reports that profits based on soy have grown from around $10 billion in the early 1990s to more than $35 billion today for Latin America. Brazil and Argentina have benefitted most from China's growing hunger for soy, with exports growing from around 25 million tons in 2000 to almost 40 million tons in 2005 – which accounts for more than half of China's total soybean imports.

China is also the world's leading importer of metal ores, a large percentage of which comes from South America. Brazil is China's third largest supplier of iron ore and largest exporter of iron ore in the world, accounting for billions of dollars in profit for Brazil. As China's need increases, so will Brazil's exports to China. Chile and Peru, the largest producers of copper in the world, account for more than 50% of China's copper imports, according to Trinh.

China's investments have been in the area of transportation, with an eye toward making resource deliveries more efficient. China is partnering with Brazil to improve Brazil's railways and establish a rail link to the Pacific to cut transportation costs of iron ore and soybeans. Other countries also are benefitting from Chinese investment. China is proposing to build a rail link in Colombia to rival the Panama Canal. The 220- kilometer line would connect Cartagena, on the northern Atlantic coast of Colombia, with its Pacific coast, making it easier for China to pass goods through Latin America and import raw materials. China is currently Colombia's second-largest trade partner after the U.S., with bilateral trade rising from $10 million in 1980 to more than $5 billion in 2010, according to The Guardian's Tania Branigan. At the same time, a consortium of three companies from China, (as well as companies from Japan and South Korea) are bidding on a high speed rail project in Brazil to connect Rio, Sao Paulo and Campinas, which shows that China's focus goes beyond the coastal countries.

In addition, China signed a $10 billion agreement with Argentina in July 2010 to refurbish two major rail lines, according to Global Intelligence Report. China signed an agreement to take a 40% stake in a Venezuelan rail project worth $7.5 billion in 2009. This project to connect oil-producing regions in Venezuela to the capital will assist China in maintaining a steady energy supply from Venezuela. There are also opportunities not paid for by China, but beneficial to the Asian country nonetheless. In January 2011, Peru completed work on a road that connects the mountainous country to Brazil. This has the potential to boost Peruvian and Brazilian trade with Asia. Peru itself has had a free trade agreement with China since 2008.

The Latin America Perspective

The expanding relationship with China is transforming Latin America. The Chinese are pursuing neighborhood relations with vigor. Thus far the idea is that China's expansive growth is both an opportunity and a threat to Latin markets. While the Chinese boom brings a positive windfall, boosting exports of Latin American countries whose endowments are commodity related, the sheer size of the growing demand presents a real challenge to Latin America. Brazil's view of China is a proper litmus test for the region as a whole. Since Brazil represents a full 50% of South American trade, it will set the standard that the region as a whole abides by when looking to China as a viable alternative to U.S. influence.

During Luiz Inacio Lula da Silva's presidency, Brazil vigorously pursued a deeper relationship with China. After the financial crisis of 2002, in which Brazil became dependent on the IMF to recover from an economic downturn, Sino-Brazilian relations became a priority for the South American nation. As this relationship blossomed, so did Chinese relations with the rest of Latin America. Now, as China becomes more deeply tied to Brazil and Latin America as a whole (Chinese FDI being greater in Latin America than any other region outside of Asia), some Brazilian officials worry that Brazil's relationship with China is presenting a large trade imbalance that could negatively affect Brazil's industries outside of agriculture and mining.

"We seek to expand the share of manufactures in exports to China," said Maria Edileuza Fontenele Reis, ambassador and Deputy Permanent Secretary for Asia at the Foreign Ministry, according to the People's Daily Online. "We seek a better position to expand our investments in China, and our interest is that China diversifies its investments in Brazil, so as to avoid excessive polarization in mining and agriculture." The ambassador made this statement before President Dilma Rousseff's first trip to China in April 2011, which focused on improving the China-Brazil bilateral relationship at the third BRICS summit.

Many in Brazil are concerned that the country's trade surplus with China masks greater problems. The concentration on commodities in Brazil's exports raises the risk of the country's agricultural growth pushing the real exchange rate and redirecting capital and labor toward the agriculture/natural resources sector at the expense of manufacturing. This is part of the reason that Brazil's currency looks so overvalued while its manufacturers are struggling to compete. This has pushed Brazil to pressure China to stop undervaluing the Yuan. China's excessive protectionism and undervalued currency has made it difficult for Brazilian companies to compete. In fact, this was one of the priorities on President Rousseff's agenda during her inaugural visit.

While these issues were not solved on the first meeting, there were steps taken to diversify China's investment in Brazil as well as Brazilian investments in China. Twenty bilateral agreements were signed between the two countries, with the largest deals coming in the areas of telecommunication, aircraft and energy, according to Latin Trade. Brazil promised to give China its long sought-after market-economy status recognition. Both sides pledged to expand and diversify investments through company partnerships. Overall, President Rousseff was pleased with the trip.

"We reached our main goals, which were to open the doors for our more sophisticated products to enter China and for working together in important fields such as science and technology," President Rousseff said upon her return to Brazil as reported by the People's Daily Online. She continued: "There's a delicate balance between 'cooperation' and 'competition' between the two sides." These concerns also are shared by the rest of the region, in order to prevent China from overwhelming local industries.

While China's commodity-based trade structure is currently lucrative, it does not encourage diversification of Latin America's exports into more value-added goods, manufactured products, and modern services. Economic relations are dependent on often unstable commodity market demands. U.S. investment in the region is far more diversified and spans a range of value-added activities, including manufacturing, finance, telecom, retail and other services. Going back to a comparison with the United States, while China accounts for 6.7% of the region's total exports, the United States continues to be the largest buyer, with a 40% share. Latin America's exports to the U.S. are more diversified and remain fairly balanced so it is better suited to survive a possible commodity cut-off in Latin America. Roughly 24% of the region's exports are raw materials, another 12% consists of resource-based goods and 60% is manufactured products. Karen Poniachik of Latin Trade also sees enormous risks for the region: "The steep overvaluation of the region's currencies—due in part to the flood of investment flows and export proceeds—is eroding the competitiveness of its higher-value added goods and services. This could in turn fuel its already high level of overdependence on commodities."

Future Implications

With both the U.S. and China making gains in the region in different sectors, there is seemingly room for each side to grow; which implies that, in fact, trade with Latin America is not a zero-sum game. China presents an alternative to the United States, but that is not necessarily a bad thing. The U.S. is much more diversified than China at the moment and therefore does not need to enter into direct competition. However, as China responds to calls from Brazil and diversifies its investments, there is increasing worry that China is going to outmatch U.S. trade in the region. These fears may be economically based, but there are potentially harmful political consequences - primarily, providing Latin America with a quasi-world power as an alternative to the U.S. Since the Monroe Doctrine, Latin America has been considered a secure sphere of influence for the U.S. The fact that China presents a less democratic alternative to U.S. influence presents a major problem.

The third BRICS summit in April provided more insight into the potential consequences of China's growing place in Latin America via its relations with Brazil. One proposal to emerge from the summit of the five nations (Brazil, India, China, Russia and South Africa) was a broad-based international reserve currency system providing stability and certainty. The idea was to set up a new exchange rate mechanism that would bypass the U.S. dollar as the reserve currency of the world. In addition, banks of the five BRICS nations agreed to establish mutual credit lines in their local currencies, not in U.S. currency. While the chances of such a proposal gaining support are debatable, it sets a clear example of a possible shift in power away from the U.S. and toward a more global organization, one that is arguably anchored by China. If China becomes a preferred partner in Latin America, it will show that U.S. dominance around the globe also is at risk.

Conclusion

So what does China's growing place in the region mean for the future? Depending on whom this question is posed to, there are two probable answers. The first is that China's intensifying relations with Latin America offer a clear sign of the end of U.S. dominance in the region, and in a greater sense, the entire world. There is enough evidence to show that the tides have changed in favor of China. The other answer is that it means nothing. The U.S. is obviously still the more dominant power in the region, and Chinese presence will eventually subside, again leaving the United States as the region's premier partner. The real answer probably falls somewhere in the middle.

Is China the preferred partner for Latin America? At this point, the definitive answer is no. However, the United States should not take its place in the region for granted. There is clear evidence of an increasingly symbiotic relationship with China throughout Latin America. While the U.S. is the most dominant trade partner to the region as a whole, it is losing ground in key countries, namely Brazil, which is blossoming on the world stage and is emerging as the clear leader in the region. Increasing trade and investment can be beneficial for all, but the power that China can derive from its growing economic influence could bring increased political and ideological influence that the U.S. might find unnerving. China already has replaced the U.S. as the largest trading partner for Brazil and Chile, and is on pace to do the same in Peru and Venezuela. At the very least, this should cause the U.S. to pay more attention to its southern neighbors and take steps to make sure that China only benefits economically and not politically at the expense of the U.S. The world will be watching.

As it stands, the Chinese are not broadening their relations with the region in a way that directly competes with the United States. China is strictly concerned with commodities, including oil. U.S. President Barack Obama recently signed an agreement with Brazil's Petrobras that will allow the oil company to drill in the Gulf of Mexico. This symbolic move could cause tensions to increase as the world's two largest oil consumers battle over rights to Brazilian oil. In that regard, the competition may go beyond a race to Latin commodities and move into the realm of fighting for political influence. It is odd to think that the United States would need to compete for hemispheric dominance with a country on the other side of the globe, but China's actions and increasing integration into the region tell us that such a scenario may one day arise. Given the proximity and importance of Latin America to the United States, this region could be the symbolic battle that best measures the continued hegemony of the U.S. versus China.

With both the U.S. and China jockeying for influence in a world where political power relations are changing, Latin America has the most to gain. The primary concern for the region is that it does not become a battle ground for a neo-Cold War between China and the U.S. Brazil already has clearly stated its concerns regarding Chinese influence. Yet, despite this tension, Brazil is now too reliant on China to turn away from the path on which Lula set the country. Agricultural exports to China are crucial to Brazil's economy. Lula's Brazil supported China politically and made clear moves away from the United States. Now Rouseff's administration has welcomed Barack Obama with open arms. With all three major actors going through stages that could influence the global economic and political landscape - China implementing its 12th five-year plan, Brazil cementing itself as a prominent world player and the U.S. still recovering from a terrible financial crisis – this dynamic relationship is one that deserves close attention from all those concerned with the future of China-U.S. relations. Where Brazil and the rest of Latin America were once looking for an alternative to U.S. influence and found China, the region may now be looking to the U.S. to strike a balance with growing Chinese influence. With the global ambitions of Latin America, namely Brazil, it is essential to maintain close ties with both the United States and China. The world will be watching.

References

Barrionuevo, A., & Romero, S. (2009, April 15). "Deals Help China Expand Sway in Latin America". *The New York Times. Retrieved March 13, 2011, from http://www.nytimes. com/2009/04/16/world/16chinaloan.html*

Branigan, T. (2010, February 14). "China goes on the rails to rival Panama Canal". *The Guardian. Retrieved March 12, 2011, from http://www.guardian.co.uk/world/2011/feb/14/china-rail-rival-panama-canal Economist. (2009, August). "The Dragon in the Backyard". The Economist, August (Week 3), pp. 12-14.*

Gallagher, K. (2010, October 2). "The Fragile bit of BRIC". *The Guardian. Retrieved March 13, 2011, from http://www.guardian.co.uk/commentisfree/cifamerica/2010/oct/01/brazil- argentina*

Global Intelligence Report. (2011, March 10). "China and Brazil Leading Energy Infrastructure Investments in Latin America". *Retrieved March 12, 2011, from OilPrice.com: http://oilprice. com/Energy/Energy-General/China-and-Brazil-Leading-Energy-Infrastructure-Investments-in-Latin-America.html*

Grant, W. (2009, September 17). "China in Huge Venezuela Oil Deal". *BBC News. Retrieved March 13, 2011, from http://news.bbc.co.uk/2/hi/8260200.stm*

Hornbeck, J. F. (2011). "U.S.-Latin America Trade: Recent Trends and Policy Issues". *Congressional Research Service Report for Congress.*

Johnson, S. (2005). "Balancing China's Growing Influence in Latin America". *The Heritage Foundation, pp. 2-5.*

McCarthy, J. (2008, April 1). "Growing Trade Ties China to Latin America". *NPR. Retrieved*

March 15, 2011, from http://www.npr.org/templates/story/story.php?storyId=89275971

MercoPress. (2011, April 2). "The delicate balance of 'cooperation' and 'competition' between China and Brazil". MercoPress. Retrieved April 11, 2011, from: http://en.mercopress. com/2011/04/02/the-delicate-balance-of-cooperation-and-competition-between-china-and-brazil

MercoPress. (2011, April 14). "BRICS calls for new global monetary system with less reliance on the dollar". MercoPress. Retrieved April 20, 2011, from: http://en.mercopress. com/2011/04/14/brics-calls-for-new-global-monetary-system-with- less-reliance-on-the-dollar

Miller, S. (2009, June 3). "Cooperating with China in Latin America". Center for American Progress Retrieved March 13, 2011, from: http://www.americanprogress.org/issues/2009/06/ cooperate_china.html

Painter, J. (2008, November 21). "China Deepens Latin America Ties". BBC News. Retrieved March 09, 2011, from: http://news.bbc.co.uk/2/hi/americas/7737554.stm

People's Daily Online. (2011, April 19). "Brazilian president says China visit productive". People's Daily Online, English Version. Retrieved April 20, 2011, from: http://english.people.com. cn/90001/90776/90883/7354361.html

People's Daily Online. (2011, March 31). "Rousseff's visit marks new phase in Brazil-China Relations. People's Daily Online, English Version. Retrieved April 11, 2011, from: http://english. peopledaily.com.cn/90001/90776/90883/7336683.html

Poniachik, K. (2011, February 07). "China's Buying Spree: Life beyond Commodities". Latin Trade. Retrieved March 15, 2011, from: http://latintrade.com/2011/02/ china%E2%80%99s-buying-spree-life-beyond-commodities

Santiso, J. (2007, July). "Can China Change Latin America?". OECD Observer. Retrieved March 12, 2011, from: http://www.oecdobserver.org/news/fullstory.php/aid/2281/Can_China_ change_Latin_America_.html

Trinh, T. (2006, June 13). "China's Commodity Hunger: Implications for Africa and Latin America". Deutsche Bank Research: China Special, pp. 2-5.

Michael Cerna is an alumnus of the International Policy Management program at Kennesaw State University, Kennesaw, GA.

Lee Teng-hui and Cross-Strait Relations: 1995-1999

Daniel S. Mojahedi
Vol. 10, No. 1
2011

Introduction

The late 1980s and early '90s saw unprecedented rapprochement between Taiwan and China. The two sides went from being at a technical state of war to having citizens from both sides visiting one another. Trade blossomed, and limited, unofficial contact between the two governments was encouraged. While Taipei and Beijing had very real and substantial differences to overcome before any official relations could be built, the confidence-building measures and growing civilian contacts did seem promising. Yet all this changed quickly. Starting in 1995, the two sides quickly backslid into a state of tension not seen for 30 years largely because of Taipei's shift away from supporting reunification with China into what Beijing perceived as clear steps toward independence.

Adding to the complexity of this shift was that the Chinese Nationalist Party, called the KMT, remained in power and was much more sympathetic to China than the opposition Democratic Progressive Party, or DPP. Any analysis as to why relations deteriorated must revolve around Taiwan's president at the time, Lee Teng-hui. As Lee and Wang note, Taiwan's cross-Strait policy during Lee's presidency was largely "a one-man show" (2003, p196), making him the central focus of any study of this time period. Thus the focus of this article is to analyze why Lee Teng-hui, head of the pro-China KMT and hand-picked successor to dictator Chiang Ching-kuo, would decide to shift away from closer ties with the mainland and seek to develop a more independent identity for Taiwan.

Cross-Strait Relations Prior to and After 1995

Before going into any detail about why Lee shifted away from the cross-Strait rapprochement of the early '90s, it is important to understand the historical context before and after 1995. Previous to 1987 any thought of rapprochement was considered treacherous. The government held fast to its "Three Noes Policy" of no contact, no negotiation, and no compromise with the CCP regime, and debate on the matter was strictly forbidden under martial law.

Yet the situation began to shift. In 1986 the DPP, which later spearheaded Taiwan's independence movement, was founded as the island's first opposition party. One year later martial law was lifted. This served as a step toward allowing the freedom of discussion needed to bring up rapprochement. It also took Taiwan off war footing toward China. In early 1988 Chiang Ching-kuo died, replaced by the island's first native Taiwanese president Lee Teng-hui. Lee continued promoting democratic principles, lifting the Period of National Mobilization for the Suppression of the Communist Rebellion in April 1991. As Roy notes, Taiwan no longer considered itself at war with China (2003, p185).

Although the war had not officially ended in Taiwan's eyes until then, the government had already begun preparing to proceed with cross-Strait relations. In January 1991 the government created the Mainland Affairs Council (MAC), a cabinet-level agency in charge of developing cross-Strait policy, along with the Straits Exchange Foundation (SEF), a quasi-private organization put in place to deal with the Chinese government as any official contact with China was still officially forbidden. The Chinese government responded in kind, creating the Association for Relations Across the Taiwan Strait (ARATS) in December of the same year. Everything was in place for contact to resume between the two sides after a 40-year hiatus.

While talks did in fact begin, and did result in technical agreements on issues such as the transfer of registered mail and the repatriation of Chinese illegal immigrants in Taiwan, practically no progress was made toward the betterment of relations between the two sides. This stagnation was due to a critical disparity in the objectives each side maintained for holding talks. The Chinese government saw the talks as paving the way for the reunification of Taiwan with China. The Taiwanese saw them as a way to normalize relations between two states (Cabestan 1998, p217) and actively avoided getting pinned down in unification talks with their Chinese counterparts.

This stagnation would turn into outright hostilities during and after 1995 as Lee Teng-hui began showing more concern for Taiwan's political reform, sovereignty, and international status at the expense of relations with the mainland. From 1995 to the end of his presidency in 2000, Lee engaged in a series of activities that served to anger and frustrate Beijing. These included a high-profile visit to the U.S. in 1995 during which Lee actively sought to promote Taiwan's interests, encouraging the island's shift from a Chinese to Taiwanese national identity through his New Taiwanese campaign, and finally his description of relations between Taiwan and the mainland as state-to-state relations. These activities brought cross-Strait tensions to a new all-time high where they would remain until Ma Ying-jeou became president in 2008.

The Political Center

Lee's shift was at least in part determined by the will of the public. As democratic reforms took hold in the early '90s the KMT began paying more and more attention to the needs and wants of the political center. According to public opinion polls conducted by the Election Study Centre of NCCU, the public had been shifting its preferences from unification to either maintaining the status quo or even independence, with just a fifth of the population supporting unification by 1995 (Election Study Centre, 2011). This put public opinion at diametric odds with the stated goals of China's bid for rapprochement. Although the KMT had long maintained its desire to reunify Taiwan with China, the political center's moderated stance could not be ignored. Lee, looking to maintain the KMT's power in a more democratic environment, embraced a broader Taiwanese identity and gradually slowed the island's rapprochement with the mainland in order to accommodate this political center.

To make matters more complicated, the KMT no longer monopolized the promotion of unification with the mainland in Taiwan's political arena. In late 1993 the New Party (NP) was founded from the New KMT faction, later pushing more aggressively for eventual unification with China. This created two factors that allowed the KMT to shift toward a more moderated stance. First of all, the exodus of many of the hardliners from the KMT to the NP removed much inner-party opposition and helped Lee consolidate his power within the KMT and pursue more liberal cross-Strait policies (Roy 2003, p188). Secondly, as the NP staked a more extreme position on the political spectrum, taking possession of this part of the electorate, the KMT was forced toward a more moderated stance (Fell 2005, p117). This proved advantageous to the KMT. Cabestan notes that, as new parties formed and staked out their cross-Strait policy, Taiwan's political theater went from having one cross-Strait policy to three (1998, p229). Finding itself on the political spectrum in between the DPP on one side and NP on the other, the KMT was now seen as a moderating force, protecting the country from two extremes and more responsive to the political center (Fell 2005, p102). Thus, because the KMT aligned itself more with the political center through its shift to one of cautious links with the mainland, Lee was both able to defend Taiwan's sovereignty against pressures from China, consolidate his power within the KMT and, as will be discussed in the next section, help the party fare better in national elections.

National Election Politics

The KMT would never be more keenly aware of the political center's position on cross-Strait issues than during national elections. For one thing, as Su points out (2004, 58-59), it is advantageous for Taiwanese candidates to be seen as the underdog. As elections draw near on the island, voters often see campaign flags and posters with the characters ??, meaning "to make an emergency rescue." Candidates want to be seen as fighting an uphill battle in order to garner as much support as possible right before the election. Lee Teng-hui was able to take advantage of this political tactic by portraying himself as an underdog standing up against a belligerent communist China during the missile crises of 1995 and 1996. The crises, during which the PLA fired missiles into the waters near Taiwan's two major ports, was a reaction by the Chinese government to a private visit by Lee to the U.S. and an attempt to warn people not to vote for him in the upcoming presidential elections. The crises caused China to be seen as the aggressor and created a defiant Taiwanese public, helping Lee soundly defeat his opponents (Su 2004, p46). As one elite interviewee pointed out to Fell, "If the CCP attacks and you do not attack back, then you'll lose. People will think that you have no guts. You are a coward (2005, p128)." Lee thus stood up to China, attacking back.

Another advantage Lee was able to reap by promoting Taiwan's sovereignty during this period was to bring cross-Strait relations to the forefront of domestic politics when the KMT was struggling to maintain public trust in other areas of domestic concern. This fact was particularly true for how the island's youth saw Lee. The younger generations within Taiwan's population do not harbor the same amount of animosity that is seen in the older generations. In fact, they tend to worry about cross-Strait relations much less than more immediate concerns such as education and employment (Rigger 2006, pp31-32), areas in which the KMT was not accomplishing as much as the public wished. In fact, many voters saw Lee's 1995 trip to the U.S. as a way to isolate himself from the KMT's failure to fight corruption (Roy 2003, p198). With his trip to the U.S., and by maintaining a brave face against China's threats, Lee was able to highlight his successes in defending Taiwan's sovereignty while also taking attention off of the KMT's failures (Fell 2005, p19), giving the electorate cause to be wary of China, and portraying himself as the brave underdog.[1] Lee was thus able to both promote Taiwan's sovereignty and consolidate his power through the island's first direct presidential elections. While, as Su points out, in the long run cross-Strait tensions would

---

1   *It is interesting to note that the results of the election closely mirrored the public's desires regarding sovereignty (Cabestan 1998, p232).*

push the political center away from independence (2004, p63), for the elections Lee's moderated stance was given the advantage.

Economic Factors

One important threat to Lee's power and Taiwan's sovereignty during the mid- to late '90s was the growing economic ties between the two sides of the strait. Although Taiwan did not officially open up to cross-Strait trade until 1987, it had been going on at least since China opened its doors in 1979 (Luo 1998, pp18-23). By 1995 this trade had grown to US$11.46 billion and by 1997 equaled 10.33% of Taiwan's total foreign trade and 7.52% of China's (Luo 1998, p17). In fact, if it had not been for Taiwan's US$16.61 billion surplus with China, the island would have suffered an overall international trade deficit of US$8.97 billion, compared to the US$7.74 billion surplus it enjoyed in reality (Luo 1998, p17). By any reckoning Taiwan and China were becoming economically integrated.

This would threaten Lee's power and Taiwan's sovereignty in two ways. First of all, it was believed that increased economic relationships between the two sides would lead to less Taiwanese animosity toward China (Rigger 2006, p7). Secondly, this closer economic integration was a threat to Lee's power by creating a unified challenge to his cross-Strait policy. While there was much disagreement about the advantages and disadvantages of cross-Strait economic ties, business leaders across the political spectrum were very much for those ties, creating a unified opposition to Lee's policies (Lee and Wang 2003, pp191-193).

Lee would work to stave off this perceived economic threat, while at the same time countering China's political and military threats, by tying economic relations to the cross-Strait political environment and trying to induce Taiwanese companies not to invest in or trade too heavily with China. As Tso notes, Lee tried to play the economic card in an attempt to force China to yield to Taiwan's economic demands (1996, pp132-133). In lieu of such political concessions, Lee sought to prevent any kind of rapprochement on China's terms that would lead to further economic integration. For example Myers and Zhang theorize that another reason Lee made his 1999 "State-to-State" comment was to derail upcoming talks and prevent the kind of mainland fever that was seen after the talks held in the early '90s (2006, pp42-43). While the KMT was indeed keen to be seen as working toward the island's economic interest, Lee was loathe to do so at the expense of his personal power and Taiwan's national interests.

Conclusion

Throughout the mid- to late '90s Lee showed clearly that he preferred to maintain Taiwan's sovereignty and his own personal power base over improving ties with China. Yet, despite the fact that Lee had his own clear ideas on how cross-Strait policy should be dictated, these ideas were not created in a vacuum. Firstly they were developed in response to the political center's wishes, which decreasingly saw the island as a province of China. Secondly they were developed as a way to politicize cross-Strait relations during national elections, namely the 1996 presidential election. Finally they were developed as a response to what Lee saw as an overheated economic integration of the two sides that would give the business community too much political sway while mollifying public opinion toward China. Many scholars question the success of Lee's cross-Strait policies, as economic ties continued to flourish and Taiwan's international space remained limited. Nevertheless, it cannot be denied that they were borne out of very real concerns regarding the island's status in the global arena that were shared by much of the public.

These factors gain much more relevance today as KMT President Ma Ying-jeou looks to re-engage China after more than a decade of chilled relations. Indeed there are some differences between what happened with Lee and what Ma faces now. However, the similarities between the two cannot be ignored. Regarding the differences, Ma has embraced the cross-Strait economic ties Lee feared and has given up the zero-sum game over diplomatic relations Lee so eagerly fought with China. On the economic front Taiwan's trade surplus with the mainland, shrinking be it may, has helped the island's sagging export-based economy, and Chinese tourists visiting the island have created a limited but real boost for local businesses. On the diplomatic front, China has responded to Ma's rapprochement by making limited concessions, such as not objecting to Taiwan's WHA membership as an observer. However, China's intentions to reunite Taiwan with the mainland remain unchanged and, despite Ma's pleading, Beijing has not renounced its willingness to take back Taiwan militarily, continuing to add to its missile arsenal aimed at the island.

The greatest similarity between the two environments is that China still expects unification between the two sides, and the majority of people on Taiwan are against any such endeavor. Ma must also function in an election system and political environment similar to what Lee faced. While much of the New Party has been re-absorbed into the KMT, Ma was put into office by an electorate whose political center has continued moving further away from a Chinese national identity and support of unification, keeping pressure on him not to make too many concessions to Beijing. In short, while tensions have been reduced during Ma's tenure, it has only eased some of the symptoms of the problem, not provided a cure. If the two sides of the Strait are going to develop any lasting rapprochement, they will have to do so in a way that will acquiesce to China's own needs to maintain its sovereignty and territorial integrity while not abandoning the island's own political and economic desires. If they do not, history could very well repeat itself, and Ma could be left facing many of the same difficult choices Lee was faced with almost two decades earlier.

Bibliography

Bridging the Straits. 2007, Jiang Zemin's Eight-point Proposal [Internet]. http://english.cri. cn/4426/2007/01/11/167@184028.htm [accessed 9 January 2008].

Cabestan, J.O. 1998, Taiwan's Mainland Policy: Normalization, Yes; Reunifation, Later. In Shambaugh, D. (ed) Contemporary Taiwan, Clarendon Press, Oxford. PP216-239.

Chao, C. 2002, The Republic of China's Foreign Relations Under President Lee Teng-hui: A Balance Sheet. In Dickson, B. and Chao, C. (eds) Assessing the Lee Teng-hui Legacy in Taiwan's Politics: Democratic Consolidation and External Relations, M.E. Sharpe, Armonk, New York. Ch. 9.

Directorate General of Customs, Ministry of Finance, ROC, 2011, Year Comparison Of Roc Imports & Exports By Continent (Area), Country (Region): K - (CNHK) Time Period : 2009/01 - 12 V.S 2008/01 - 12 [Internet] Available at: http://cus93.trade.gov.tw/ENGLISH/ FSCE/ [accessed 21 February 2011].

Election Study Center, NCCU. 2011, Important Political Attitude Trend Distribution [Internet]. http://esc.nccu.edu.tw/english/modules/tinyd2/content/tonduID.htm [accessed 21 February 2011].

Fell, D. 2005, Party Politics in Taiwan: Party change and the democratic evolution of Taiwan, 1991-2004, Routledge, London.

Kuo, J. 2002 Cross-Strait Relations: Buying Time Without Strategy. In Dickson, B. and Chao, C. (eds) Assessing the Lee Teng-hui Legacy in Taiwan's Politics: Democratic Consolidation and External Relations, M.E. Sharpe, Armonk, New York. Ch. 10.

Lee, W. and Wang, T (eds) 2003, Sayonara to the Lee Teng-hui Era: Politics in Taiwan, 1988-2000, University Press of America, Lanham, Maryland.

Myers, R. and Zhang, J. 2006, The Struggle Across the Taiwan Strait: The Divided China Problem, Hoover Institution Press, Stanford, California.

Rigger, S. 2006, Taiwan's Rising Rationalism: Generations, Politics, and "Taiwanese Nationalism." Policy Studies, 26.

Roy, D. 2003, Taiwan: a political history, Cornell University Press, Ithaca, New York.

Sheng, L. 2002, China and Taiwan: Cross-Strait Relations Under Chen Shui-bian, Zed Books, London.

Su, C. 2004, Driving Forces Behind Taipei's Mainland Policy. In Tsang, S. (ed) Peace and Security Across the Taiwan Strait, Palgrave Macmillan, New York. Ch. 3.

Tso, A. 1996, Developments in the Cross-Strait Economic Relationship. Issues and Studies, 32.9.

Daniel Mojahedi graduated from the School of Oriental and African Studies in London and lived in Taiwan for several years.

Vietnam's Relations with China: A Delicate Balancing Act

Dennis C. McCornac

Vol.10, No.2
2011

The agreement between China and Vietnam on the process to guide the settlement of maritime issues signed in October 2011 may be a first step in easing tensions over the contentious issue of who controls the islands in potentially oil-rich waters which China calls the South China Sea and Vietnam calls the East Sea. The establishment of a hotline between the two countries' capitals to resolve crises and the creation of semiannual talks are aimed at finding "mutually acceptable basic principles" and a long-term approach to solving maritime disputes. The two countries are now committed to friendly consultations to properly handle maritime issues and make this area a sea of peace, friendship and cooperation.[1]

China and Vietnam share a long history marked by collaboration and cordiality, but also tumult and hostility at times, as far back as the first century B.C., and as recently as during the last half-century. Nevertheless, following modern economic reform in China and Doi Moi in Vietnam, both countries have continued on their transition path to a market-oriented economy putting industrialization and trade issues at the forefront, with territorial disputes generally left on the back burner. The year 2010 marked the 60th anniversary of the establishment of China-Vietnam diplomatic ties with official normalization of relations being in place since 1990. There is no doubt that China and Vietnam will forever be intertwined because of geographic, economic and political realities.

---

1   Tuoi Tre News, *"China sign agreement on basic sea principles,"* 12 October 2011. *http:// www.tuoitrenews.vn/cmlink/tuoitrenews/politics/vn-china-sign-agreement-on-basic-sea-principles-1.47607*

Swinging on a Tightrope

A Vietnamese government official once described Vietnam as swinging on a tight-rope in which China held one end and the United States held another. Not willing to place all its eggs in either basket given its past history with both nations, and in an effort integrate into the global economy, Vietnam is pursuing a foreign policy of what some analysts label "more friends, fewer enemies." Stable, normalized economic and military relations with both China and the United States are the current state of affairs. Vietnam has also placed an emphasis on global integration which has resulted in political and economic engagement with a wider range of countries, the purpose which is presumed to counter the influence of Beijing in the region.

Strains in Sino-Vietnamese relations emerged in 2009 when China presented a claim to 80 percent of the South China Sea (East Sea) to the United Nations Convention on the Law of the Sea. This put Vietnam in the awkward position of either accepting Chinese dominance of this areas or risking an engagement.[2]

The issue is particularly important to both sides since it involves the claim on possession of two island groups: the Paracels and Spratlys. The most important matter at stake is who has the right to explore and exploit the natural resources in and below the waters surrounding the islands. Although proven reserves have not yet been forthcoming, the most optimistic estimates from China suggest potential oil resources of the Spratly and Paracel Islands could be as high as 213 billion barrels of oil and the area is also rich in natural gas.[3]

The disputes will ultimately focus on who has the rights to these natural resources, and is being structured as a legal dispute on the interpretation and application of Article 121 of the 1982 United Nations Convention on the Law of the Sea (UNCLOS). Article 121 provides that an island - defined as "a naturally formed area of land above water at high tide" - can, in principle, generate the same maritime zones as land territory. These include a 12 nautical mile (nm) territorial sea; a 200 nm exclusive economic zone (EEZ) and a continental shelf.[4]

Some of the Spratly Islands' features claimed and occupied by China and Vietnam, and other countries as well, do not meet the definition of an island. In addition, a majority of the declared EEZs overlap, and historical claims to ownership are difficult to prove. As Jörn Dosch notes, "Outcomes are unpredictable given that all claimants have at least some convincing arguments on their side...yet Beijing holds the key to a resolution of the dispute which will either be decided through Chinese power projection or a negotiated settlement on the Chinese

---

2   Sophie Quinn-Judge, "Vietnam and China: Shoals ahead," *openDemocracy,* 29 April 2010.
    http://www.opendemocracy.net/sophie-quinn-judge/vietnam-and-china-shoals-ahead
3   U.S. Energy Information Administration, "South China Sea - Analysis brief," 16 June 2011.
    http://www.eia.gov/countries/regions-topics.cfm?fips=SCS.
4   Robert Beckman, Islands or rocks? Evolving dispute in South China Sea. RSIS Commentaries,
    10 May 2011. http://www.rsis.edu.sg/publications/Perspective/RSIS0752011.pdf

terms. The latter seems more likely than the former.[5]

It is not, however, in the best interest of Vietnam to antagonize China un-necessarily. Ideologically, Vietnam is more comfortable with China than with the United States. Economically, China is a large market, a source of financial assis-tance and a model of development.[6] Nevertheless, in Vietnam as well as China, nationalist sentiments have put pressure on their governments to remain firm on issues of sovereignty. For Hanoi, the matter has become especially sensitive as an array of dissidents has taken up the cause of the archipelagoes, accusing the ruling Communist Party of selling out to China with every act of acquiescence.[7]

A controversial mining venture involving China in 2009, for example, al-though supported by the Vietnamese Communist Party, raised the ire of notable figures in Vietnam, including military icon General Vo Nguyen Giap. "I would like to propose to the prime minister to stop the implementation of bauxite ex-ploitation until its ecological impact is seriously studied by international experts," wrote the 97-year-old retired general, criticizing the agreement allowing China to mine and process bauxite in the central highlands region.

The project was divisive for a number of reasons with critics contending it would leave behind scarred landscape and produce effluents that pollute farmland and water sources. The central highlands are well known for production of coffee and other crops that are important sources of export earnings. Complicating the matter was the announcement that China would be bringing in its own workers to run the project, raising the specter of a permanent Chinese settlement in this strategically sensitive area. Originally thought to be an economic boom to the region, only a few jobs for Vietnamese workers were in the plans, causing outcries of Chinese economic imperialism and colonization.

Although the early phase of construction of the bauxite mine began in March of 2010, the issue may have more serious political implications for Vietnam in the long run. The unwavering support for the project by the majority of the most powerful members of the Vietnamese Communist Party has been attributed by some to payoffs to these officials by the Chinese. And the government of Prime Minister Nguyen Tan Dung was accused of kowtowing to China and selling out to Beijing and to capitalism.

A new concern in Vietnam, attributed to the "Chinese economic expansion," is represented by the influx of illegal Chinese laborers, particularly involving joint

5   Jörn Dosch, "The Spratly Islands dispute: Order-building on China's terms?" *Harvard Inter-national Review*, 18 August 2011. http://hir.harvard.edu/the-spratly-islands-dispute-order-building-on-china-s-terms?page=0,1

6   Hung Nguyen, "Vietnam," *The Diplomat*. http://the-diplomat.com/whats-next-china/vietnam/ Accessed 30 September 2011.

7   Ishaan Tharoor, "China and Vietnam: Clashing over an island archipelago, "*TimeOnline*, 14 January 2010. http://www.time.com/time/world/article/0,8599,1953039,00.html

Vietnam - China projects. Vietnamese press and labor leaders have warned of the irregular situation of Chinese workers in Vietnam. According to statistics from the Ministry of Labor, War Invalids and Social Security, in May 2011 there were 74-thousand foreign workers in Vietnam and among these employees, 90 percent are Chinese. Most Chinese employees, it is argued, do not have professional skills and the workers are causing instability in the economic, social, military, political spheres as well as everyday life of people. Newly elected President Truong Tan Sang has spoken out and told Vietnamese authorities and employers to better manage the country's foreign workforce.[8]

The Dragon is Awake and Hungry

Despite the occasional hiccup, China and Vietnam bilateral relations are becoming more interdependent, particularly in the realm of economics. The year 2010 marked the 60th anniversary of the establishment of Sino-Vietnamese diplomatic ties, with official normalization of relations being in place since 1990. This has led to a rush of political goodwill and a boom in economic trade evidenced by growth in bilateral trade jumping from US$32 million in 1991 to just a shade below US$28 billion in 2010 and for the first nine months of 2011, it rose by 35 percent as compared with the same period of the previous year (See Figure 1).

China is Vietnam's largest trade partner (See Figure 2), but because of China's size and global trade integration, Vietnam counts for less than one percent of

Figure 1: China-Vietnam Bilateral Trade and Trade Balance

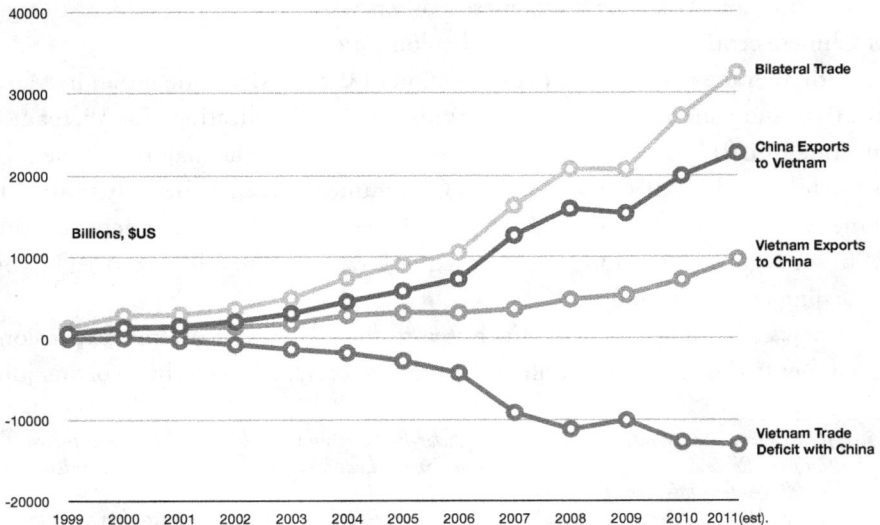

---

8   *Thanh, Nien Weekly,* "President encourages stricter management of foreign labor," 12 August 2011. http://www.thanhniennews.com/2010/Pages/20110813150236.aspx

Figure 2: Vietnam's Major Trading Partners in 2010 (percent of total trade)

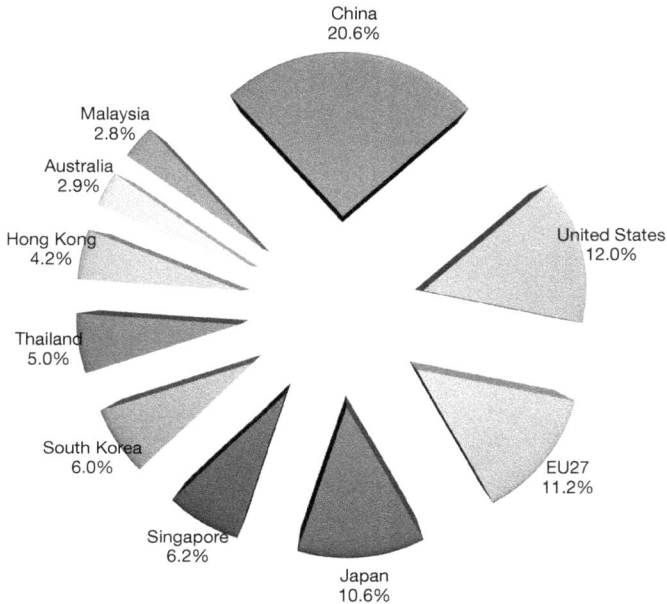

China
20.6%

Malaysia
2.8%

Australia
2.9%

Hong Kong
4.2%

United States
12.0%

Thailand
5.0%

South Korea
6.0%

EU27
11.2%

Singapore
6.2%

Japan
10.6%

source: IMF (DoTS) DG Trade European Union 27 Members

China's total export trade.

Bilateral trade is increasing at a significant rate particularly, because China's insatiable demand for goods and resources. Sustaining economic growth for a nation reaching almost 1.4 billion citizens requires a tremendous amount of natural resources, much of which needs to be imported. As China scours the globe building economic relationships with various nations and regions to ensure a continuous supply of commodities such as coal, crude oil and iron ore, it is only natural to look to a close neighbor for help.[9] Further spurring trade, particularly along Vietnam's northern border with China, has been the establishment of the Free Trade Area (FTA) between China and 10 member states of the Association of Southeast Asian Nations (ASEAN) that took effect January 1, 2010.[10]

The size of bilateral trade notwithstanding, Vietnam's trade deficit with China is continuously rising, with Vietnam selling unfinished commodities and running a trade deficit with China of more than US$12 billion in 2010. This figure is expected to rise substantially for the foreseeable future. The discrepancy in the trade balance can be attributed mainly to the types of products Vietnam exports to China: coal, crude oil, rubber, foodstuff, seafood and footwear, to name a few

9   Joyce Roque, "*Resources, relations and free trade: How China is opening up its borders to Vietnam, China Briefing, 10 December 2007. http://www.china-riefing.com/news/2007/12/10/resources-relations-and-free-trade-how-china-is-opening-up-its-borders-to-vietnam.html.*

10 People's Daily Online, "*Effect of China-ASEAN Free Trade Area turning protruding, 30 March 2010. http://english.peopledaily.com.cn/90001/90780/91344/6935005.html.*

Figure 3: Vietnam Exports to China (January-September 2011)

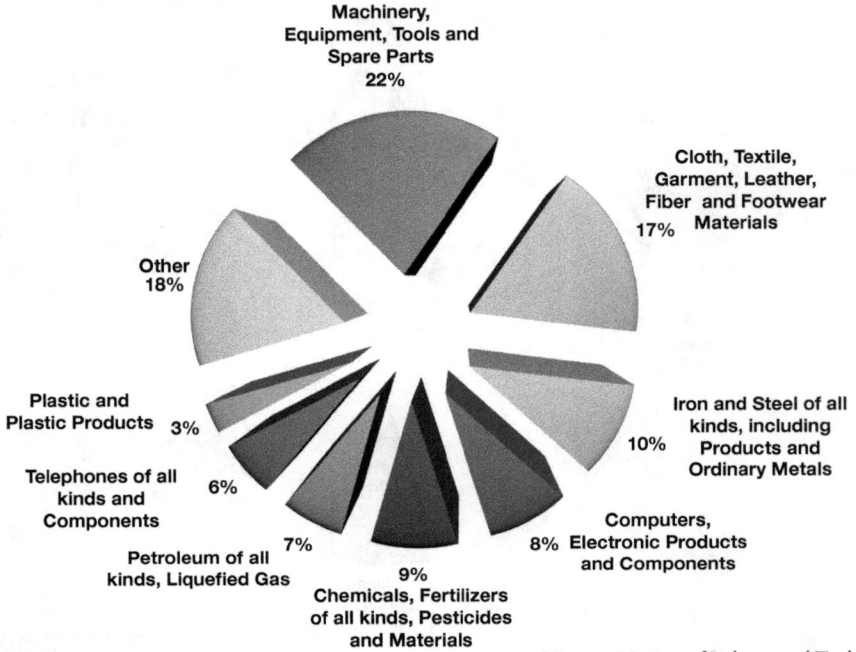

source: *Vietnam Ministry of Industry and Trade*

(See Figure 3). The majority are either raw materials or low-value-added manufactured goods.

On the other end of the spectrum, China's top exports to Vietnam include high-value-added manufactured goods such as cars, motorbike parts, machinery, package equipment, pharmaceuticals and petroleum (See Figure 4). China, for example, accounts for almost 60 and 17 percent of Vietnam's coal and oil export revenue respectively, and is also the major importer of natural rubber needed to fuel China's industrial rubber products industry.

Currently, there are almost 2,000 China-funded firms in Vietnam engaged in trade and investment, project contracting and other businesses. Vietnamese enterprises are paying more attention to the Chinese market and are looking to China for more business opportunities and markets for selling equipment and raw materials. China is also a main market for Vietnam tourism, accounting for one-fourth of the international tourists to Vietnam (almost 786,000 arrivals) in the first seven months of 2011. While the opening of markets and trading routes can be described as a win-win situation for China and Vietnam, it may be too simple a formula precisely because of the disparities between the two countries, particularly in terms of economic size and political power.[11]

---

11   Brantly Womack, China-ASEAN pact offers more than win-win, AsiaTimes, 7 January 2010.
     http://www.atimes.com/atimes/China_Business/LA07Cb01.html

Figure 4: Vietnam Imports from China (January-September 2011)

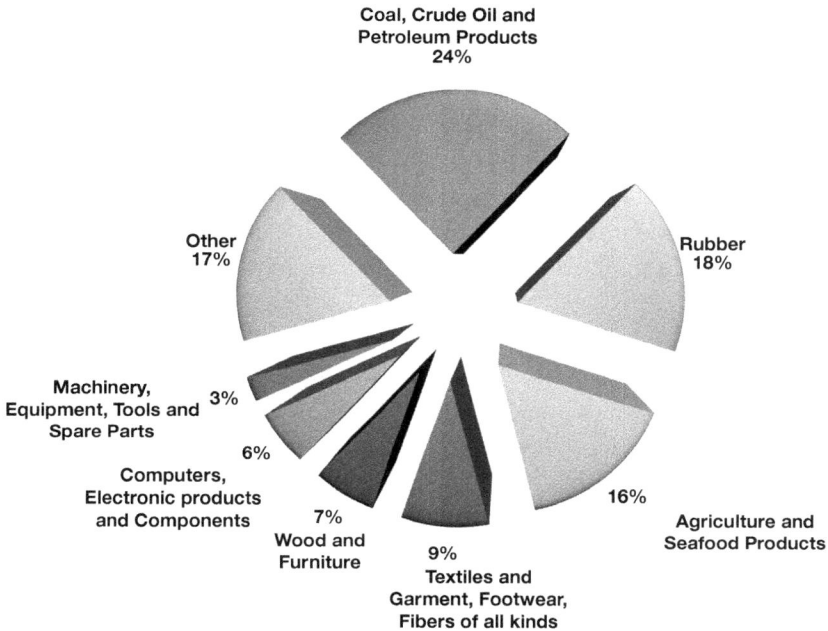

Coal, Crude Oil and
Petroleum Products
24%

Rubber
18%

Other
17%

Machinery,
Equipment, Tools and   3%
Spare Parts

6%

Computers,
Electronic products
and Components

16%

7%
Wood and
Furniture

Agriculture and
Seafood Products

9%
Textiles and
Garment, Footwear,
Fibers of all kinds

source: *Vietnam Ministry of Industry and Trade*

The influx of Chinese goods, both smuggled over the border and imported legally into the Vietnamese market, has negatively impacted the domestic production of a number of goods in Vietnam, particularly consumer goods. One special concern in Vietnam is that many of the goods are of low quality and dubious origin and may contain toxins and other substances harmful to people's health. Some products can be made in Vietnam, but are still imported as the latter approach is more cost-effective. This, in turn, has choked a host of Vietnamese enterprises, including production of chopsticks and toothpicks.[12]

Truong Thi Thuy Lien, director of the Lien Phat Ltd. Company, a shoe manufacturer in southern Vietnam, notes that since early 2011, prices of materials imported from China have increased by 40 percent against the end of 2010, exposing sudden price increases as the biggest risk factor in such imports. Economic expert Le Dang Doanh said local producers imported a large quantity of material from China because the country was nearby, so transport costs were low and added incentive for domestic exporters.[13]

Further adding to uncertainty regarding the pricing of Chinese imports is China's

12   VietnamNet, "Economists give alerts about increasing invasion of Chinese imports," 21 May 2011. http://english.vietnamnet.vn/en/print/business/8489/economists-give-alerts-about-increasing-invasion-of-chinese-imports.html

13   Vietnam News, "Reliance on imports poses risks, " 22 August 2011, http://vietnamnews.vnagency.com.vn/Economy/214600/Reliance-on-imports-poses-risks.html

overall trade surplus, which has escalated tensions with a number of its trading partners who are now arguing that the Chinese currency, the Yuan, is undervalued. Should China revalue its currency, Vietnam would see import prices rising even faster, putting more inflationary pressures on an economy with already escalating prices.

Even though this dependence on increasingly expensive Chinese imports has already pushed many Vietnamese firms into the red, Vietnam's heavy dependence on trade with China is only expected to increase over time. Le Hong Hiep of the Vietnam National University fears that "should China decide to discontinue trade with Vietnam for some reason, the damage to Vietnam's economy would be immense.[14]

Wither the Future

Relations between China and Vietnam have improved recently, and the conciliatory nature of the recent meeting between Beijing and Hanoi has ushered in a relative period of calm. Both countries appear keen to continue to foster better bilateral ties and improvements in Sino-Vietnamese relations are unlikely to damage Vietnam's relations with the U.S.

However, anytime China swings the tightrope more aggressively, Vietnam finds itself in a more precarious position, not knowing which end of the rope is the safest point of refuge. If the Vietnamese government is to continue to be successful in maintaining a balance, it must avoid too close an alignment with one country at the expense of ties with the other.

Now is a relatively unique time in Vietnam's history. It is unified, and it has the economic and political wherewithal to challenge China in the region - though whether it will be successful remains to be seen.[15] The rise of national sentiments on either side may portend more troubling times ahead. And as a Vietnamese diplomat is quoted as saying, "No one will say it openly, but what drives every meeting in Southeast Asia now is fear of what the region will be like with China dominating."[16]

Dennis McCornac teaches at Loyola University Maryland, Baltimore, Maryland.

---

14 Le Hong Hiep, "Vietnam: Under the weight of China," East Asia Forum, 27 August, 2011. http://www.eastasiaforum.org/2011/08/27/vietnam-under-the-weight-of-china

15 Stratfor, Global intelligence, "Vietnam, China: Economic prosperity leads to heightened tensions," October 5, 2011. http://www.stratfor.com/memberships/202836/analysis/20111004-vietnam-china-economic-prosperity-leads-heightened-tensions

16 Joshua Kurlantzick, "After Deng: On China's transformation," The Nation, 27 September 2011. http://www.thenation.com/article/163669/after-deng-chinas-transformation

China's Increasingly Assertive Navalism

John Garver
Vol. 10, No. 1
2011

The turmoil in Libya that began in February 2011, together with the need to evacuate an estimated 30,000 Chinese from that country, led to the deployment of a PLA-N frigate to the eastern Mediterranean. The 4,000 ton warship, commissioned only in 2008 and deployed to anti-pirate duty off Somalia, could not carry many evacuees. But it could stand guard over possible attempts to disrupt the evacuation. China's Commerce Ministry reported that at least 27 Chinese-run construction sites in Libya had been attacked by armed individuals and that there were numerous injuries.[1] China has been compelled a number of times to evacuate its citizens from war zones: Kuwait in 1990 and Iraq in 2003, for instance. But Libya in 2011 was the first time China had used military assets to protect such an evacuation. Chinese guns standing offshore would make malfeasants on shore think twice.

This was only the most recent demonstration of the naval aspect of China's current rise. China is increasingly operating in seas far from home and using naval power in support of a range of objectives. In November 2010, 100 ships and 1,800 PLA Marines participated in live fire exercises in the South China Sea. Viewed by 200 military observers from foreign countries, the exercises came after U.S. Secretary of State Hillary Clinton had suggested a U.S. role in resolving the South China Sea territorial dispute and as Southeast Asian countries were moving to strengthen their claim to islands and seabed resources in that region. According to one PLA analyst quoted by Beijing's Global Times newspaper: "It's time to

---

1   *"China dispatches warship to protect Libya evacuation mission," China Sign Post, 24 February 2011. http://www.chinasignpost.com*

oppose these interventions with power politics."[2]

A month earlier PLA warships made their first-ever public visit to Myanmar ports. The visit by a two warships was part of a multi-country tour. Chinese warships have been visiting ports in the Indian Ocean since 1985, and Chinese warships reportedly have occasionally called at Myanmar's ports before. But the 2010 visit was the first publicly announced visit. Indeed, the occasion was celebrated by the Chinese ambassador as well as representatives of Chinese companies, teachers, and students based in Myanmar.[3]

In 2007 China launched its first ship built specially to serve as a hospital ship.[4] Such ships play a central role in humanitarian assistance and disaster relief ("HA/DR" in naval jargon) that has become a mainstay of U.S. naval diplomacy during the post-Cold War period. According to Xinhua, China's new hospital ship made it one of only a few countries in the world to possess long-range medical capabilities. The PLA-N hospital ship undertook its first exercise in March 2009, visiting Chinese military outposts in the South China Sea. Chinese analysts made clear that the main mission of the new hospital ship was to support amphibious attack operations. The year before the hospital ship was commissioned, China launched its largest indigenously designed amphibious assault ship to date.[5] With a 20,000 ton displacement the vessel delivers assault forces by hovercraft and helicopters.

The most substantively important PLA-N deployment came in 2008 when Chinese warships were deployed to the Gulf of Aden to protect against pirate attacks. This was the first time the PLA-N had undertaken sustained and complex operations at great distances from China. Such an accomplishment is crucial to true naval capability – as opposed to simply having an impressive list of naval hardware. One friend at the China Maritime Studies Center of the U.S. Naval War College made a comparison to the British and French fleets during the epic battle at Trafalgar in 1804; while the British seamen literally lived at sea for months on end and were excellent at related skills, French seamen were bottled up in their harbors and seldom were able to put to sea for more than a few days at a time. Only sustained sea operations at great distance and under varied conditions generate true naval capability. Chinese seamen are now acquiring this off Somalia.

The PLA-N is fielding new and potent naval warfare systems. Chinese shipyards recently began producing several new classes of submarines and frigates qualitatively more capable than earlier PLA-N warships.[6] Early in 2010 the U.S.

2   "China Stages Naval Exercises Where Tensions with Its Neighbors have Grown," New York Times, 4 November 2010, p. A6.
3   "Chinese Navy Warships Make first Visit to Myanmar," Xinhua, 29 Aug. 2010.
4   "China's Growing Maritime HA/DR Capabilities," China Brief, vol. x, no. 12 (11 June 2010), p. 5-7.
5   "China's new large amphibious assault ship," International Assessment and Strategy Center, 8 January 2007. http://www.strategycenter.net
6   The People's Liberation Army Navy; A Modern navy with Chinese Characteristics, Office of

Office of Naval Intelligence reported advanced Chinese work on anti-ship ballistic missiles, probably based on indigenized Russian technology and designed to target U.S. aircraft carriers.[7] While developing the capability to deny U.S. carriers access to the seas around Taiwan, China is starting to build its own carriers. Late in 2010 the final paragraph of a report by the State Oceanic Administration revealed that the previous year China's government had decided to build an aircraft carrier.[8]

Commentary in PLA publications indicates that a more expansive definition of China's national interests parallels the growth of Chinese naval capabilities. Or at least some in the PLA believe this should be the case. An article in Jiefangjun Bao in March 2011 cited the recent and successful PLA-protected evacuation of Chinese nationals from Egypt and Libya to argue that China's traditional concept of limiting use of military power to defend China's own territory was inadequate to the era of globalization.

In today's age, national interests have already surpassed the traditional territorial land, sea, and air, and expanded toward the oceans, space, and even intangible information space. Interests in these domains have become important components of national interests and security of these domains has become an important content of national security. The scope touched upon by national security is not only limited to traditional 'territorial land borders'…. Maintaining normal overseas economic relations and links, protecting the security of energy, resources, and transport channels, and protecting the interests of citizens and legal entities overseas and the just rights and interests of overseas Chinese are important issues related to the overall…national development and the basic interests of the people.[9]

One of the fundamental precepts of the Realist approach to politics is that interests expand as capabilities do, and this may be what is happening now. As China develops globe-spanning naval capabilities, it may be discovering that it has globe-spanning interests to be protected by those expanding capabilities. There is nothing unusual about this; China is following the path of most other states that became naval powers.

China's embrace of navalism will make Sino-U.S. relations more complex. Until recently China had been essentially a continental, land power while the United States has been essentially a maritime power. The PRC's primary security concerns have had to do with deterring aggression against its land mass (from the U.S. in

---

Naval Intelligence, August 2009. *http://www.oni@nmic.navy.mil*

7   Andrew Erickson, "Ballistic trajectory; China develops new anti-ship missile," *Jane's Intelligence Review, February 2010. http://www.jir.janes.com*

8   "China's plan for first aircraft carrier emerges in obscure official report," *Financial Times, 13 December 2010.*

9   Huang Kunlun, "The Concept of National Interests in an Age of Globalization," *Jiefangjun Bao online, 24 March 2011, World News Connection, http://wnc.dialog.com*

Korea or Southeast Asia, or from the USSR), while the United States has typically drawn its defense perimeter through the Western Pacific chain of islands lying off the East Asian coasts. There were exceptions to this – South Korea for the U.S., Taiwan for the PRC – but the big picture held. A sort of geographic division thus underlay the spheres of influence of the two powers, and this fact was cited by writers, especially Robert Ross of Boston College, to argue that the PRC and the U.S. were likely to work out a mutual accommodation. Now Chinese and U.S. spheres overlap more.

One gloomy case study contemplated by scholars is Anglo-German rivalry in the early 20th century. Historical analogies are never conclusive, but they can sometimes be suggestive. Britain's global position was based essentially on maritime power, while Prussia-Germany commanded the preeminent army on the continent of Europe. The cautious Chancellor Otto von Bismarck understood this and deliberately eschewed construction of a big navy that would challenge Britain and drive it into alignment with Germany's nemesis, France. Emperor Wilhelm II fired Bismarck and developed a High Seas Fleet that could challenge Britain's navy. Germany's navalism was a major factor pushing Britain toward alignment with France against Germany and, by extension, unleashing World War I.

China, and indeed the whole world, was blessed by a giant statesman like Deng Xiaoping. Deng's Bismarck-like prudence and realism has thus far underlain the PRC-U.S. comity underpinning China's peaceful rise. Let us hope there are not unintended consequences to China's embrace of naval power.

John Garver, Ph.D. is professor of international relations at the Sam Nunn School of International Affairs, Georgia Institute of Technology, Atlanta, Georgia.

About the Editors

Penelope B. Prime: Beginning with her first visit to China in 1976, Dr. Prime has more than 30 years of experience studying the dynamic Chinese economy. After majoring in Chinese studies and studying Mandarin as an undergraduate, she earned a Ph.D. in economics at the University of Michigan. Dr. Prime is currently Professor of International Business in the Institute of International Business, J. Mack Robinson College of Business, Georgia State University, and Director of the China Research Center. Dr. Prime's research focuses on China's economy and business environment, including topics such as China's foreign trade and investment, domestic market reforms, and provincial and local-level development, as well as applied business and economics cases on China and Asia. Her most recent books are *Global Giant: Is China Changing the Rules of the Game?* (co-edited with Eva Paus and Jon Western, Palgrave McMillan, 2009) and *Taiwan's Democracy: Economic and Political Challenges*, (co-edited with Robert Ash and John W. Garver, Routledge, 2011).

James R. Schiffman: Dr. Schiffman is Assistant Professor in the Mass Communication Department at Georgia College & State University in Milledgeville, Georgia. Previously, he served as Chief Copy Editor at CNN International, where he was involved in editorial decision making, network style, hiring, and training. Prior to joining CNN, Dr. Schiffman was a staff correspondent for *The Wall Street Journal* in Atlanta and *The Asian Wall Street Journal* in Hong Kong, Seoul, and Beijing. As a correspondent in Beijing between 1986 and 1988, Dr. Schiffman reported extensively on Chinese economic reforms, the role of foreign investment, and Chinese politics and culture at a time of rapid change and turmoil. Dr. Schiffman speaks Mandarin Chinese, and lectures occasionally to academic and community groups. He earned a Ph.D. in Communication at Georgia State University in May 2012 and is the editor of *China Currents*, the online journal of the China Research Center.